MW01166866

To Jennifer:

You are all my reasons, I love you...

All inquiries, suggestions and comments should be addressed to the Worldwide Distributor:

RUSH Publications and Educational Consultancy, LLC

1251 N Miller Rd, Scottsdale, AZ 85257

United States

Author	:	Ruşen MEYLANİ
e–mail	:	rusen.meylani@asu.edu; meylani@superonline.com
phone	:	+1 480 884 1597

All graphics and text based on TI 83 – 84 – 89 have been used with the permission granted by Texas Instruments.

From: Bassuk, Larry < l–bassuk@ti.com >
Sent: Thursday, February 27, 2002 16:23 PM
To: Meylani, Rusen < meylani@superonline.com >; Foster, Herbert < h–foster@ti.com >; Vidori, Erdel < e–vidori@ti.com >
RE: USAGE OF TI 83 + FACILITIES IN MY SAT II MATH BOOKS
Rusen Meylani,
Again we thank you for your interest in the calculators made by Texas Instruments.
Texas Instruments is pleased to grant you permission to copy graphical representations of our calculators and to copy graphics and text that describes the use of our calculators for use in the two books you mention in your e–mail below.
We ask that you provide the following credit for each representation of our calculators and the same credit, in a way that does not interrupt the flow of the book, for the copied graphics and text:
Courtesy Texas Instruments
Regards,
Larry Bassuk
Copyright Counsel
972–917–5458

————Original Message————
From: Bassuk, Larry
Sent: Thursday, February 21, 2002 9:14 AM
To: 'Rusen Meylani'; Foster, Herbert
Subject: RE: USAGE OF TI 83 + FACILITIES IN MY SAT II MATH BOOKS
We thank you for your interest in TI calculators.
I am copying this message to Herb Foster, Marketing Communications Manager for our calculator group. With Herb's agreement, Texas Instruments grants you permission to copy the materials you describe below for the limited purposes you describe below.
Regards,
Larry Bassuk
Copyright Counsel
972–917–5458

————Original Message————
From: Rusen Meylani [mailto:meylani@superonline.com]
Sent: Wednesday, February 20, 2002 5:57 PM
To: copyrightcounsel@list.ti.com – Copyright Legal Counsel
Subject: USAGE OF TI 83 + FACILITIES IN MY SAT II MATH BOOKS
Dear Sir,
I am an educational consultant in Istanbul Turkey and I am working with Turkish students who would like to go to the USA for college education. I am writing SAT II Mathematics books where I make use of TI 83 + facilities, screen shots, etc. heavily. Will you please indicate the copyright issues that I will need while publishing my book?
Thanks very much in advance. I am looking forward to hearing from you soon.
Rusen Meylani.

From: Pam Bentley [mailto:pbentley@enc.org]
Sent: Wednesday, August 04, 2004 6:21 PM
To: rushco@superonline.com
Subject: SAT II Math with TI

Good morning.

I am writing from the **Eisenhower National Clearinghouse**. **ENC** is funded by the **US Department of Education** as a place **to bring quality math and science products** together **under one roof**. We let our teacher audience know about these products through our website, www.enc.org.

Our Mathematics Content Specialist saw your book **SAT II Math with TI** on your website and would like to **add it to our collection**. Would you consider sending a review copy to me at the address below?

Once here, ENC staff will build a descriptive record and export that record to our site. Teachers can then search the site and all orders are referred back to the publisher/distributor.

I invite you to browse our site and let me know if I can answer any questions. Teachers have come to rely on ENC for product information. During our last bi – monthly period over 30,000 simple searches were recorded from our curriculum resources pages.

Thanks very much.

Pam Bentley

Acquisitions Specialist
ENC
1929 Kenny Road
Columbus, OH 43210 – 1079
614–688–3265
pbentley@enc.org
www.enc.org

Our greatest glory is not in never falling but in rising every time we fall.

CONFUCIUS

ACKNOWLEDGMENTS

I would like to thank the students from USA, Turkey and all other countries for their helpful comments, suggestions and encouragement; I have made sure we have observed them all.

I would like to thank Mustafa Atakan ARIBURNU, my ex–student and my lifetime friend for believing in me and for his continuous support.

I would like to thank TEXAS INSTRUMENTS for providing scientists and mathematicians such powerful hand – held computers, the TI family of graphing calculators. With these wonderful machines, teachers of mathematics can go beyond horizons without the need to reinvent the wheel all the time. I would also like to thank TEXAS INSTRUMENTS for providing me with a limited copyright to use the graphs that have been produced by the TI 83 – 84 – 89 Family of graphing calculators throughout this book.

I would like to thank Eisenhower National Clearinghouse (formerly funded by the US Department of Education) for adding this very book in their catalogue in order to let the math educators know about it.

I would like to thank Erdel VIDORI of TEXAS INSTRUMENTS for his suggestions on the organization and title of this book as well as his invaluable efforts in establishing the link between myself and TEXAS INSTRUMENTS.

I would like to thank Zeynel Abidin ERDEM, the chairman of the Turkish – American Businessmen Association (TABA) for his valuable support and contributions on our projects.

I would like to thank Emel UYSAL and Seda EREN for their valuable contributions.

I would like to thank Pınar ERKORKMAZ for her excellent work on the cover design.

I would like to thank Yorgo İSTEFANOPULOS, Ayşın ERTÜZÜN, Aytül ERÇİL, Bayram SEVGEN, Zeki ÖZDEMİR, and Nuran TUNCALI for whatever I know of analytical thinking.

I would like to thank my mother and my father for being who I am.

Last but not the least, I would like to thank Jennifer CHINN (MEYLANI), my soon to be wife, for saving me from the despair I used to be in, not long ago; and for her continuous and unconditional support. Therefore I dedicate this book to her.

The best way out is always through.

Robert FROST

TABLE OF CONTENTS

Some men see things as they are and say 'Why?';

I dream of things that never were and say 'Why not!'

Robert Francis KENNEDY

PREFACE

What do you see in the picture above? A Picasso

How about this one? A Meninas

SAT II Math with TI 89

Can you see the Meninas behind the Picasso?

A seemingly easy mathematical problem can be as complicated as the Picasso:

$$x^2 = e^x - 2$$
$$x = ?$$

How do you solve for x?

Solution:

- Find the Taylor series expansion of e^x and get the first few terms, possibly the first three terms and solve the quadratic equation that results.
- Use iterative methods such as Newton – Raphson but be careful with chosing your initial value.

Problem of accuracy??? What do you think!

In fact, high school students (juniors NOT seniors) in the world are expected to solve such equations (check the SAT math level 2 subject tests).

Do high school students learn Taylor series or Newton Raphson? NO! except for the ones who get advanced calculus courses.

A novel approach for the solution:

$$x^2 = e^x - 2$$

Since we have the technology, why not just ask the calculator to solve it for you!

Solve($x^2 = e^x - 2$, x)
OR
Sketch the graph of $y = x^2 - e^x + 2$
and find its x intercept!

x = 1.319:
Simpler, more accurate,
AND
"easier to teach and learn!"

"The Meninas behind the Picasso!"

"Being able to see the Meninas behind the Picasso!"
THIS IS WHAT BRINGS SUCCESS IN LIFE.

Nothing in life is as crystal clear as the Meninas. Things often appear as complicated as the Picasso. Those who can see the Meninas behind the Picasso will move forward. Those who fail to do so will have to remain insignificant!

SAT II Math with TI 89

This book is the extended and revised second edition of the legendary "SAT II Math with TI" intended to help high school students who are bound to take either or both of the SAT Mathematics Level 1 and Level 2 Subject tests. This book is devoted to the usage of the **TI–89** family of graphing calculators in the context of **Algebra, Pre–Calculus and SAT Mathematics** with hundreds of carefully designed and fully solved questions. In this edition there is an additional chapter that analyses the **TI–89** calculator inside out along with **2 full length original sample tests**, one for the SAT Math Level 1 Subject Test and the other one for the SAT Math Level 2 Subject Test; each one comes with its answer key and a typical score conversion table.

The method proposed in this book has been developed through 5 years' experience; has been proven to work and has created a success story each and every time it was used, having helped hundreds of students who are currently attending the top 50 universities in the USA, that include many Ivy League schools as well.

The main advantage of the approach suggested in this book is that, **YOU CAN SOLVE, ANY TYPE OF EQUATION OR INEQUALITY** with the TI, whether it is algebraic, trigonometric, exponential, logarithmic, polynomial or one that involves absolute values, **WITHOUT NEEDING TO KNOW THE RELATED TOPIC IN DEPTH** and having to perform tedious steps; you can solve all types of equations and inequalities very easily and in a very similar way **JUST NEEDING TO LEARN A FEW VERY EASY TO REMEMBER TECHNIQUES.** But there are still more to what you can do with the TI; find period, frequency, amplitude, offset, axis of wave of a periodic function, find the maxima minima and zeros as well as the domains and ranges of all types of functions; perform any operations on complex numbers, carry out any computation involving sequences and series, perform matrix algebra, solve a system of equations for any number of unknowns and even write small programs to ease your life. More than 20 of the 50 questions in the SAT Math Subject tests are based on these topics. This is why the method proposed in this book promises to raise the SAT Mathematics Subject test scores by at least 200 points.

The topics that are listed above are typically what a student learns at high school algebra classes. This book is intended to fulfill the need for a book specifically designed for an college bound high school senior who wishes to score perfectly on the SAT math subject tests in a very short period of time. It is very important that a student follows the order in the book step by step, there is nothing more or nothing less than what a student must learn; each and every question is unique. A wise student must aim at finishing them all, trying to capture the methods suggested.

As a final word for the college bound senior: Please do keep in mind, that **if you can give yourself to mathematics, mathematics will give you the world**. So, best of luck while getting prepared…

Ruşen MEYLANİ.

Those who do not wish to get any rest never get tired.

Mustafa Kemal ATATÜRK

INTRODUCTION

Mathematics Level 1 and Mathematics Level 2 are the two subject tests that the College Board offers. Both tests require at least a scientific, preferably a graphing, calculator. Each test is one hour long. These subject tests were formerly known as the Math Level IC and Math Level IIC subject tests.

Mathematics Level 1 Subject Test

Structure: A Mathematics Level 1 test is made of 50 multiple choice questions from the following topics:
- Algebra and algebraic functions
- Geometry (plane Euclidean, coordinate and three – dimensional)
- Elementary statistics and probability, data interpretation, counting problems, including measures of mean, median and mode (central tendency.)
- Miscellaneous questions of logic, elementary number theory, arithmetic and geometric sequences.

Calculators in the Test

Approximately 60 percent of the questions in the test should be solved without the use of the calculator. For the remaining 40 percent, the calculator will be useful if not necessary.

Mathematics Level 2 Subject Test

Structure: A Mathematics Level 2 test also is made of 50 multiple choice questions. The topics included are as follows:
- Algebra
- Geometry (coordinate geometry and three – dimensional geometry)
- Trigonometry
- Functions
- Statistics, probability, permutations, and combinations
- Miscellaneous questions of logic and proof, elementary number theory, limits and sequences

Calculators in the Test

In Math Level 2, 40 percent of the questions should be solved the without the use of the calculator. In the remaining 60 percent, the calculator will be useful if not necessary.

Which calculator is allowed and which is not

The simplest reference to this question is this: No device with a QWERTY keyboard is allowed. Besides that any hand held organizers, mini or pocket computers, laptops, pen input devices or writing pads, devices making sounds (Such as "talking" computers) and devices requiring electricity from an outlet will not be allowed. It would be the wisest to stick with TI 84 or TI–89. Both of these calculators are easy to use and are the choices of millions of students around the world who take SAT exams and also university students in their math courses. It is very important to be familiar with the calculator that you're going to use in the test. You will lose valuable time if you try to figure it out during the test time.
Be sure to learn to solve each and every question in this book. They are carefully chosen to give you handiness and speed with your calculator. You will probably gain an extra 150 to 200 points in a very short period of time.

6# SAT II Math with TI 89

IMPORTANT: Always take the exam with fresh batteries. Bring fresh batteries and a backup calculator to the test center. You may not share calculators. You certainly will not be provided with a backup calculator or batteries. No one can or will assist you in the case of a calculator malfunction. In such cases, you have the option of notifying the supervisor to cancel your scores for that test. Therefore, always be prepared for the worst case scenario (Don't forget Murphy's Rules.)

Number of questions per topics covered

The following chart shows the approximate number of questions per topic for both tests.

Topics	Approximate Number of Questions	
	Level 1	Level 2
Algebra	15	9
Plane Euclidean Geometry	10	0
Coordinate Geometry	6	6
Three – dimensional Geometry	3	4
Trigonometry	4	10
Functions	6	12
Statistics	3	3
Miscellaneous	3	6

Similarities and Differences

Some topics are covered in both tests, such as elementary algebra, three – dimensional geometry, coordinate geometry, statistics and basic trigonometry. But the tests differ greatly in the following areas.

Differences between the tests

Although some questions may be appropriate for both tests, the emphasis for Level 2 is on more advanced content. The tests differ significantly in the following areas:

Geometry

Euclidian geometry makes up the significant portion of the geometry questions in the Math Level 1 test. Though in Level 2, questions are of the topics of coordinate geometry, transformations, and three – dimensional geometry and there are no direct questions of Euclidian geometry.

Trigonometry

The trigonometry questions on Level 1 are primarily limited to right triangle trigonometry and the fundamental relationships among the trigonometric ratios. Level 2 places more emphasis on the properties and graphs of the trigonometric functions, the inverse trigonometric functions, trigonometric equations and identities, and the laws of sines and cosines. The trigonometry questions in Level 2 exam are primarily on graphs and properties of the trigonometric functions, trigonometric equations, trigonometric identities, the inverse trigonometric functions, laws of sines and cosines. On the other hand, the trigonometry in Level 1 is limited to basic trigonometric ratios and right triangle trigonometry.

Functions

Functions in Level 1 are mostly algebraic, while there are more advanced functions (exponential and logarithmic) in Level 2.

Statistics

Probability, mean median, mode counting, and data interpretation are included in both exams. In addition, Level 2 requires permutations, combinations, and standard deviation.

In all SAT Math exams, you must choose the best answer which is not necessarily the exact answer. The decision of whether or not to use a calculator on a particular question is your choice. In some questions the use of a calculator is necessary and in some it is redundant or time consuming. The only angle mode in Level 1 is degree. Be sure to set your calculator in degree mode by pressing "Mode" and then selecting "Degree." However, in Level 2 you must decide when to use the "Degree" mode or the "Radian" mode. There are figures in some questions intended to provide useful information for solving the question. They are accurate unless the question states that the figure is not drawn to scale. In other words, figures are correct unless otherwise specified. All figures lie in a plane unless otherwise indicated. The figures must NOT be assumed to be three – dimensional unless they are indicated to be. The domain of any function is assumed to be set of all real numbers x for which f(x) is a real number, unless otherwise specified.

Important Notice on the Scores

In Level 1 questions the topics covered are relatively less than those covered in the Level 2 test. However, the questions in the Level 1 exam are more tricky compared to the ones in Level 2. This is why if students want to score 800 in the Level 1 test, they have to answer all the 50 questions correctly. But in the Level 2 test, 43 correct answers (the rest must be omitted) are sufficient to get the full score of 800.

Scaled Score	Raw Score in Level 1 Test	Raw Score in Level 2 Test
800	50	43
750	45	38
700	38	33
650	33	28
600	29	22
550	24	16
500	19	10
450	13	3
400	7	0
350	1	−3

There are two ways of spreading light, to be the candle or the mirror that reflects it.
Edith WHARTON

CHAPTER 1.

TI–89 BASICS

Mathematics is a language.

Josiah Willard GIBBS

SAT II Math with TI 89

1.1 Turning the TI–89 On and Off

In order to turn on the TI–89, press the (ON)^OFF key. In order to turn off the TI–89 press the (2ND) key followed by the

(ON)^OFF key.

1.2 Resetting Memory

Resetting the memory will restore the initial factory settings that are the default settings of the calculator as well as

clear the memory. The required key combination is (2ND) (6)^MEM N.

1.3 Restoring the Default Settings

This may be necessary when the default calculator settings have to be retrieved in a single step after changing mode

settings, screen settings, etc. The required key combination is (2ND) (6)^MEM N.

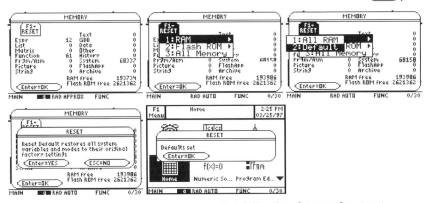

1.4 Adjusting Screen Contrast

When the calculator is reset, it will retain its factory settings, which sometimes cause the screen to have non – ideal

contrast adjustment. In order to achieve proper contrast adjustment: Press the (2ND) key followed by the (▲) or the

(▼) keys to darken or lighten the screen.

1.5 The Math Menu

Most of the built in commands that will be used in the SAT math subject tests context, that don't exist as separate

keys or key combinations, can be found in the **MATH** menu, followed by the left, right, up or down arrows. The **MATH**

main

screen can be accessed by pressing the (5)^MATH M key and looks like the following:

The **Number** menu looks like the following:

The **List** menu looks like the following:

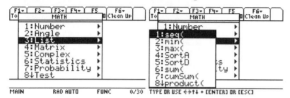

The **Matrix** menu looks like the following:

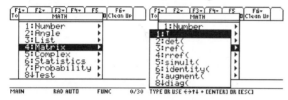

The **Complex** menu looks like the following:

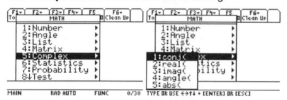

The **Statistics** menu looks like the following:

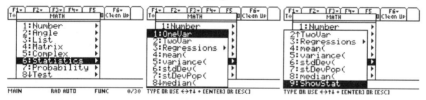

The **Probability** menu looks like the following:

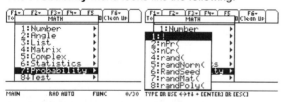

The **Test** menu looks like the following:

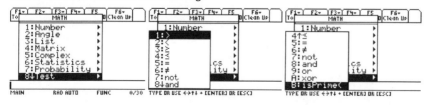

The **Algebra** menu looks like the following and it can also be accessed using the $\boxed{F_2}$ key:

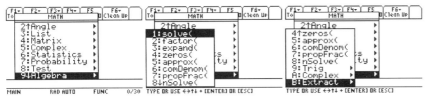

All necessary trigonometric functions can be accessed through the key combinations when possible, **CATALOG** or the **Trig** submenu of the **Algebra** menu.

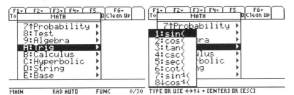

1.6 The CATALOG

The catalog contains all of the built in expressions and functions. It can be accessed by pressing the 2nd key followed by the (CATALOG) key that will serve as the **CATALOG** command. Pressing any key that contains a capital letter on the right hand corner (without the **ALPHA** key) will take you to the beginning of the portion of the catalog whose initial is that letter. For example after the catalog is opened, pressing the **SIN** key will take you to the beginning of the commands staring with the letter Y. After this point the arrows followed by **ENTER** may be used to select the appropriate command. **CATALOG** can be accessed when the exact location of a certain expression or command is forgotten.

1.7 Exact and Approximate Answers

TI–89 has the valuable option of providing the user with exact or approximate answers. These options are accessible through the $\boxed{\text{MODE}}$ key.

The default option is **AUTO** where the calculator will attempt to give the exact answer unless the calculation involves a decimal number; when there is no decimal involved, pressing the $\boxed{\blacklozenge}$ $\overset{ENTRY\;\approx}{(\text{ENTER})}$ key combination will yield the approximate answer.

For instance: 24/99 followed by the $\overset{ENTRY\;\approx}{(\text{ENTER})}$ key in the **AUTO** mode will give in the following result:

However, 24/99 followed by the key combination in the **AUTO** mode will give in the following result:

The exact answer involves fractions such as $\dfrac{2}{9}$, roots such as $\dfrac{\sqrt{3}}{2}$, trigonometric expressions such as $\dfrac{3\pi}{4}$ and the like. Although this is a superior facility of TI–89 and can be handy sometimes, it can also increase the calculation time and become unpractical especially when the answers are given approximately (which is usually the case in SAT mathematics subject tests.) Moreover, when the calculator is in the **AUTO** mode, the [♦] (ENTRY ≈ ENTER) key combination will be needed whenever an approximate answer is needed. Therefore we recommend that the calculator be in the **APPROXIMATE** mode unless an exact answer is really required.

1.8 PEMDAS (order of operations) is observed with the TI

Parentheses
Exponents
Multiplication
Division
Addition
Subtraction

PEMDAS is the correct mathematical order of operations, which is observed with the TI. Therefore you do not need to open redundant parentheses and complicate simple mathematical expressions. Any correct mathematical expression will be calculated correctly subject to the **PEMDAS** rule.

For instance $10 + 2 \cdot 3^2 - 9^{(2+1)} / 18 - 2$ must be input as follows:

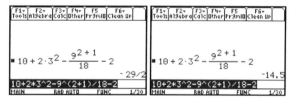

On the other hand, $4/3\pi$ will be assumed by TI as $\dfrac{4}{3}\pi$ and not as $\dfrac{4}{3\pi}$.

When $\dfrac{4}{3\pi}$ is meant it must be input as $4/(3\pi)$; in such case the use of a parenthesis will be absolutely necessary.

Similarly $4/3\sqrt{2}$ will be assumed by TI as $\dfrac{4}{3}\sqrt{2}$ and not as $\dfrac{4}{3\sqrt{2}}$.

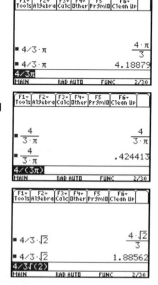

When $\dfrac{4}{3\sqrt{2}}$ is meant it must be input as $4/(3\sqrt{2})$; in such a case the use of a

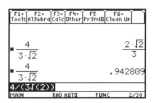

parenthesis is necessary.

1.9 Editing Expressions

Any expression can be edited using a combination of the following keys:

The **CLEAR** key when pressed on a line will clear that line. In any case of error (2ND) key followed by the

(ESC) key will serve as the **QUIT** command. The (←) key will serve as backspace when pressed alone;

when followed by the (2ND) key, it serves as the **INS** (insert) key and it may be used to insert an expression

exactly before the position of the cursor. In order to position the cursor, a combination of the left, right, up, down arrows can be used. It is also possible to **CUT**, **COPY** and **PASTE** expressions using the appropriate key combinations.

1.10 The ANS Variables

The last answer after the enter key is pressed is stored in the variable **ans**:

The **ans** variables are updated whenever the enter key is pressed. If there is an operation associated with the **ans** variable or if there is an expression involving the **ans** variable prior to pressing the enter key, the output will be changed each time the enter key is pressed. For example if the last expression entered is **ans − 5** and the last answer is 4, pressing the enter key once again will produce −1, which is the last answer decreased by 5. This allows the user to perform a stream of operations followed one after another.

1.11 Accessing a Previous Entry

In order to access previous entries that you have made, for each retrieval, use the (◀)(▶) (▲) (▼) keys

followed by the (ENTER) key. This will retrieve the previous entries in the screen since the last reset. Please note

that there is a limit to the number of calculations stored on the screen depending on the memory (RAM) available. Please also note that the content if the **ANS** variables may be modified each time the enter key is pressed.

1.12 The Operational Minus Sign and the Number Minus Sign

The number minus sign	The operational minus sign

The TI has two minus keys, which are often confused. The one on the left hand side above is the number minus sign and it will be used while writing $(-3 + 4)^2$. The one on the right hand side is the operational minus sign and it must be used when writing $(3-4)^2$. These two keys mixed up may lead to syntax errors or which is worse, calculation errors and incorrect answers.

1.13 The Display Digits

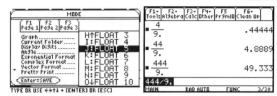

The **Display Digits** menu accessed by the MODE key determines the number of significant digits displayed. Please note that this does not necessarily mean the number of decimal digits that are displayed although they are also affected by the display digits. Please also note that the displayed answer is not actually changed by the calculator by a rounding off operation. The number of significant digits is 5 in the above display, however the actual results that are stored in memory still have the maximum number of decimal points. The display is changed only, the results are not altered at all. The default option is **Float 6**.

1.14 Storing Values in a Variable

In the above calculation, $3+\sqrt{2}$ is stored in X and $X^2 + 2X$ is evaluated. In order to do this operation the following key combination must be used:

$3+\sqrt{2}$ (STO▶) X

You can also store different numbers in different variables and work accordingly:

For example X = 3.7824 and Y = $2\pi - 3$ and you are required to calculate $\dfrac{X^2 - XY}{X + Y^3}$.

In this case you should do the following with the TI:

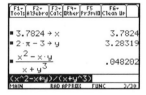

1.15 Storing a Single–variable or a Multi–variable Function

A valuable facility of TI–89 is the fact that it can perform symbolic manipulations. In the following examples we define the single–variable functions f(x) = $\dfrac{x \cdot \sin(x)}{\ln(x)-3}$ and g(x) = $x^2 + \dfrac{\tan(x)}{1-3x}$ and perform the calculations f(3), g(2π − 3) and

g(f(2π − ln(3))) = (gof)(2π − ln(3)) where gof is the composite function g(f(x)).

In the following example we define the two variable function

$h(x, y) = \dfrac{x + y}{xy + \ln(xy)}$ and calculate $h(3\pi - 2, e^3)$ where e is

Euler's constant, the irrational number that approximately equals 2.71828.

The following example shows the calculation of $h(f(3),$

$g(\pi - 1))$ where $f(x) = x^3 + 2x^2 + 4$, $g(x) = \dfrac{x \cdot \sin(x)}{x + 2}$ and

$h(x, y) = x^2 \cdot y + x \cdot y^2$

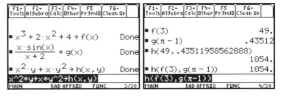

Any stored value or function will remain in the calculator system until it is rewritten or erased directly or by resetting the calculator.

1.15 Square Roots, Cube Roots, n'th Roots, Fractional Powers

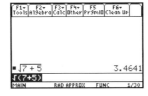

$\sqrt{7 + 5}$ must be input as follows:

Please note that unlike TI 83 – 84 all opened parenthesis need to be closed.

$\sqrt[3]{9^2}$ can be input in as:

Please be careful with how you enter $9^{\frac{2}{3}}$. 9^2/3 would mean $(9^2)/3$ and not $9^{\frac{2}{3}}$ or $9^{2/3}$. $9^{\frac{2}{3}}$ must be entered as 9 9^(2/3).

1.16 Operations on Complex Numbers

On the first hand please note that TI–89 can calculate any expression that involves the imaginary number i, where $i^2 = -1$ or $i = \sqrt{-1}$ regardless of its mode of operation. However, if a non–real operation is to be carried out, the calculator mode must be set to one of the **RECTANGULAR** or the **POLAR** formats in the Complex Format submenu accessible through the **MODE** key. When the Complex Format is set to **REAL**, $\sqrt{-1}$ will be interpreted as a non real result:

When the Complex Format is set to **RECTANGULAR** or **POLAR**, $\sqrt{-1}$ will be interpreted correctly:

The **RECTANGULAR** option will display a complex result in the form a + bi where a and b are real numbers. The **POLAR** option will display the result in the form r · e$^{i\theta}$ where r is the magnitude and θ is the angle of the complex number a + bi; please note that e$^{i\theta}$ = cos(θ) + i · sin(θ) by Euler's famous identity.

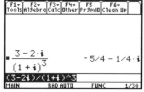

$\dfrac{(3-2i)}{(1+i)^3}$ must be input as follows:

Other operations that are commonly needed in the SAT II Math context are as follows:

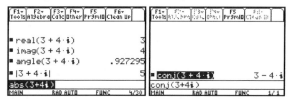

The required functions can be found at the **MATH Complex** submenu:

1.17 Built in functions in TI–89 that are commonly used in SAT II Math

The commonly used trigonometric functions required for the SAT math subject tests context are as follows:

FUNCTION	DESCRIPTION
sin(	Sine function
cos(	Cosine function
tan(	Tangent function
cot(	Cotangent function
sec(	Secant function
csc(	Cosecant function

The commonly used inverse trigonometric functions required for the SAT math subject tests context are as follows:

FUNCTION	DESCRIPTION	ALSO KNOWN AS
sin^{-1}(	Arcsine or sine inverse function	Arcsin
cos^{-1}(	Arccosine or cosine inverse function	Arccos
tan^{-1}(	Arctangent or tangent inverse function	Arctan
cot^{-1}(	Arccotangent or cotangent inverse function	Arccot
sec^{-1}(	Arcsecant or secant inverse function	Arcsec
csc^{-1}(	Arccosecant or cosecant inverse function	Arccsc

The remaining commonly used functions required for the SAT math subject tests context are as follows:

FUNCTION	DESCRIPTION
10^(	
e^(	
log(	Logarithm base 10
ln(	Logarithm base e
$\sqrt{(}$	Square root
abs(	Absolute value
int(	Greatest integer function

As an example $\dfrac{1+3\ln 2}{4-3\cdot e^5}$ is input as follows:

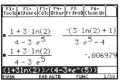

All of the above functions can be found in the **MATH** menu.

1.18 Additional Functions

If you need to define the following functions (such as when you are using an old TI–89 that does not have the functions in the MATH menu or the CATALOG, you can use the following definitions:

WHEN YOU NEED	USE THE FOLLOWING DEFINITION	WARNING
sec(x)	1/cos(x)	
csc(x)	1/sin(x)	
cot(x)	cos(x)/sin(x)	Although mathematically correct, still DO NOT USE 1/tan(x) for cot(x) because when tan(x) is undefined, TI will interpret 1/tan(x) as undefined, too, which is not correct.
$\sec^{-1}(x)$	$\cos^{-1}(1/x)$	Do NOT use $1/\cos^{-1}(x)$, mathematically incorrect.
$\csc^{-1}(x)$	$\sin^{-1}(1/x)$	Do NOT use $1/\sin^{-1}(x)$, mathematically incorrect.
$\cot^{-1}(x)$	$\pi/2 - \tan^{-1}(x)$ if in radians $90° - \tan^{-1}(x)$ if in degrees	Do NOT use $1/\tan^{-1}(x)$, mathematically incorrect.
$\log_a x$	log(x)/log(a) ln(x)/ln(a)	Either of these definitions can be used but please be careful with closing the parentheses that are automatically opened when **LOG** or **LN** are pressed.

As an example $\log_2 3$ can be input in one of the following ways:

However, we recommend that you use **LN** = ln(since it is accessible as a key; if you would like to use log(instead, you will need to retrieve it through **CATALOG** or **MATH** menus.

1.19 Radian and Degree

RADIAN mode interprets angle values as radians and answers displayed are also in radians.

DEGREE mode interprets angle values as degrees and answers displayed are also in degrees.

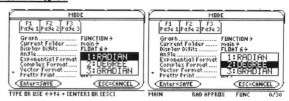

It is also possible to input angles in degrees using the degree sign ° when in radian mode or in radians using the radian sign ^{r} when in degree mode.

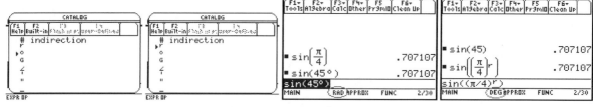

1.20 The numbers " e " (Euler's constant) and " π " (pi)

The number π can be input by the following key combination: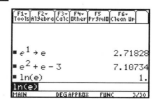

The number e can be defined as follows and it will remain in the calculator system unless it is rewritten or erased directly or by resetting the calculator.

1.21 Factorial Notation, Permutations and Combinations

n! = The product of all consecutive integers starting with 1 up to and including n that is:

$n! = n \cdot (n - 1) \cdot (n - 2) \cdot (n - 3) \ldots 3 \cdot 2 \cdot 1$

$\dfrac{(5+4)!}{5!-3!}$ can be input as follows:

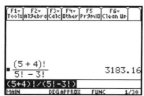

P(n, r): Number of permutations of r elements chosen from n elements where $r \leq n$; $P(n, r) = \dfrac{n!}{(n-r)!}$

C(n, r): Number of combinations of r elements chosen from n elements where $r \leq n$; $C(n, r) = \dfrac{n!}{(n-r)! \cdot r!}$

P(8, 3) and C(8, 3) can be input respectively as follows:

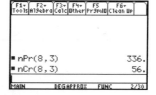

The required functions can be found at the **MATH PROBABILITY** menu:

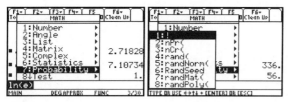

1.22 Sequences and Series

The TI has the built in feature of **seq(** command in the **LIST** menu that can be accessed through the $\boxed{\textbf{MATH}}$ key.

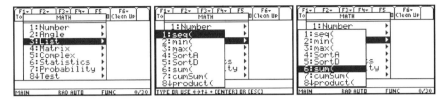

The **seq(** command will be used to generate the terms of a sequence with the following method of usage:

seq(the formula for the sequence, the variable of the sequence, the starting value for the variable, the ending value for the variable, the increment)

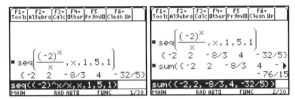

In the previous example the following inputs were used:

the formula for the sequence: $\dfrac{(-2)^x}{x}$

the variable of the sequence: x

the starting value for the variable: 1

the ending value for the variable: 5

the increment: 1

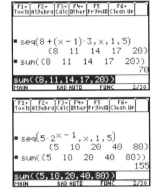

Please remember that for arithmetic sequences the formula for the sequence must be input as **a + (x − 1) · d** where **a** is the first term of the sequence and **d** is the common difference between a term and the next. For example for the sequence 8, 11, 14, 17, 20, … the formula for the sequence will be: **8 + (x − 1) · 3**

Please also remember that for geometric sequences the formula for the sequence must be input as **a · r$^{(x − 1)}$** where **a** is the first term of the sequence and **r** is the common ratio between a term and the next. For example for the sequence 5, 10, 20, 40, 80, … the formula for the sequence will be: **5 · 2$^{(x − 1)}$**

1.23 Operations on Matrices, Determinants

In order to perform operations on matrices, the user needs to define them first using the main screen and then perform the necessary operations. Let us assume that we are creating a 3 by 3 matrix A given by $\begin{bmatrix} a_{11} & a_{12} & a_{13} \\ a_{21} & a_{22} & a_{23} \\ a_{31} & a_{32} & a_{33} \end{bmatrix}$.

This matrix can be defined as follows: [a$_{11}$, a$_{12}$, a$_{13}$; a$_{21}$, a$_{22}$, a$_{23}$; a$_{31}$, a$_{32}$, a$_{33}$] $\boxed{\text{STO} \blacktriangleright}$ a

While entering the matrices, the following keys will be necessary: $\boxed{,}$ $\boxed{\div}$ $\boxed{9}$

Any special matrix operation can be found using the **MATH Matrix** submenu accessible through the MATH key:

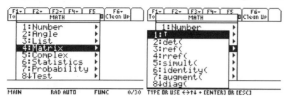

Let us work on the following illustrative example to demonstrate what we mean:

Example: 2 by 2 Matrices

If $A = \begin{bmatrix} 1 & 4 \\ -1 & 2 \end{bmatrix}$ $B = \begin{bmatrix} 0 & -1 \\ -3 & 4 \end{bmatrix}$ then find

a. $A + B$

b. $A - B$

c. $2A - 4B$

d. $A \cdot B$

e. $B \cdot A$

f. A^{-1}

g. B^{-1}

h. $A^{-1} \cdot B$

i. $B^{-1} \cdot A$

j. $\det(A)$

k. $\det(B)$

Solution:

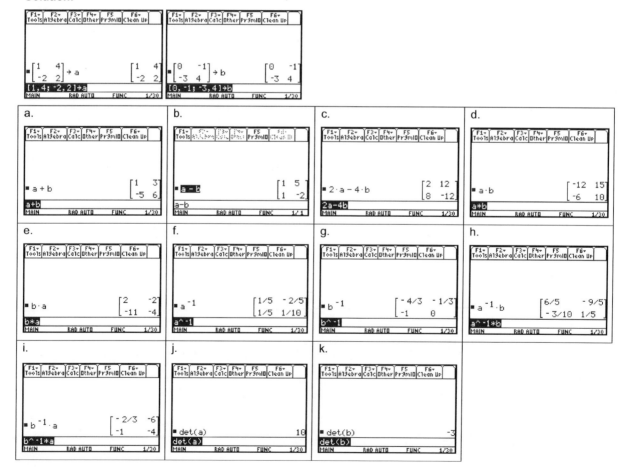

Example: 3 by 3 Matrices

Find the determinant and inverse of the matrix $\begin{bmatrix} 1 & 4 & 3 \\ -2 & 2 & 1 \\ 0 & 0 & 2 \end{bmatrix}$

Solution:

Although we will see later that any system of linear or nonlinear equations can be solved using the **F₂ Algebra** routines of TI–89, it is possible to solve a system of linear equatios very easily using the **rref(** operation on the augmented matrix or by matrix inversion. This might be useful when the **F₂ Algebra** routines are costly in terms of time and effort. Let us elaborate this on the following system of equations:

$x + y + z = 6$

$2x - y + z = 3$

$x + 2y + 3z = 13$

Solution by **rref(** operation on the augmented matrix:

The last column of the matrix that results after the **rref(** operation gives the solution set, namcly:

$x = 7/5; \ y = 11/5; \ z = 12/5.$

We could also solve the above system as follows:

Step 1: Define the matrix of coefficients **c**.

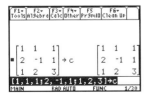

Step 2: Define the matrix of results **r**.

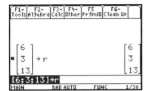

Step 3: Compute the variables by $\mathbf{c^{-1} \cdot r}$.

1.24 Statistical Applications

Before we start, please make sure that you have the flash application entitled **Statistics with List Editor App for the TI–89 Titanium**. If not, you will need to install this application; in order to be able to do so, you will need the TI Connect Software, download the application from the following link and transfer it to your calculator. We strongly suggest that you download and install the latest operating system for your TI–89.

http://education.ti.com/educationportal/downloadcenter/SoftwareList.do?website=US&tabId=1&panelId=4

Statistics of Data

Before performing any statistical calculations, it is essential to note that the data may be given in two ways, in raw format or in data – frequency format. When data is given in raw format, all data should be entered in a list named L_1. When data is given in data – frequency format, the data is entered in the list named L_1 and the individual frequencies are entered in the list named L_2. When data is in raw format, the command of **OneVar L_1** will calculate the statistics of the data and **ShowStat** will display a large portion of the the resulting statistics. Using the ⊙ will display the rest of the statistics. When data is in data – frequency format, the command of **OneVar L_1, L_2** must be used to calculate the statistics of the data. The necessary commands are accessible through the MATH Statistics menu or the flash application entitled **Statistics with List Editor App for the TI–89 Titanium**:

The calculated statistics and their meanings are as follows:

$\bar{x}$	: The arithmetic mean of the data.	nStat	: number of data
$\sum x$	: Sum of all individual entries in the data set.	minx	: Minimum entry in the data set.
$\sum x^2$	: Sum of the squares of all individual entries in the data set.	q_1	: Lower Quartile
		MedStat	: Median
Sx	: The sample standard deviation.	q_3	: Upper Quartile
σx	: The population standard deviation.	maxX	: Maximum entry in the data set.

Example:

Find the statistics of the following data: 1, 3, 5, 6, 3, 6, 6.

Solution:

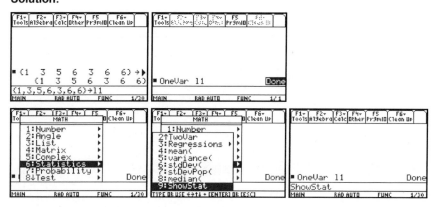

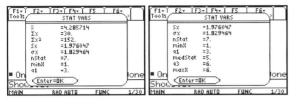

OR

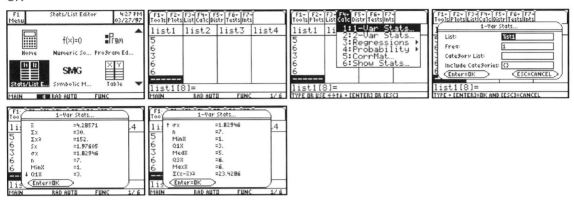

Example:

Compute the statistics of the following data:

Data	1	3	5	6
Frequency	1	2	1	3

Solution:

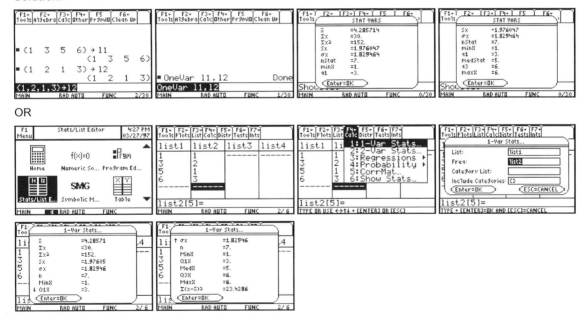

OR

Normal Distributions

Suppose we are given the mean and standard deviation of a group of data. In the context of SAT math subject test, particularly the level 2, we might be required to determine the following:

- the probability that a randomly chosen item has a value that is greater than a certain value,
- the probability that a randomly chosen item has a value that is less than a certain value,

- the probability that a randomly chosen item has a value that is between two certain values, or

- given the probability, we might be required to find what the certain value or what those values are.

In this case we will use the two very useful utilities that are accessible though the flash application entitled **Statistics with List Editor App for the TI–89 Titanium**

These utilities are **normalcdf(** and the **invNorm(**. The **normalcdf(** utility can be used in the following two ways:

- **normalcdf(lower limit, upper limit, mean, standard deviation)** or

- **normalcdf(lower limit, upper limit)**

In the latter case, the **normalcdf(** utility assumes the mean of 0 and the standard deviation of 1. The **normalcdf(** utility allows us to compute the probability that a randomly chosen item has a value that is greater than a certain value, or the probability that a randomly chosen item has a value that is less than a certain value, or the probability that a randomly chosen item has a value that is between two certain values,

Similarly, the invnorm(utility can be used in the following two ways:

- **invNorm(probability, mean, standard deviation)** or

- **invNorm(probability)**

In the latter case, the **invNorm(** utility assumes the mean of 0 and the standard deviation of 1.

Please go over the following illustrative examples:

Example:

In Geniuseum Academy, the IQ's of the students are randomly distributed with the mean of 125 and the standard deviation of 12. Perform the following calculations:

a. The probability that a randomly selected student has an IQ that is greater than 135.

b. The percentage of students whose IQ's are between 120 and 140.

c. The percentage of students whose IQ's are less than 110.

d. It is given that 80 percent of the students have an IQ that is greater than x; what is the value of x?

Solution:

a.

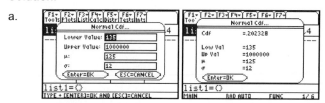

Answer: 0.2

b.

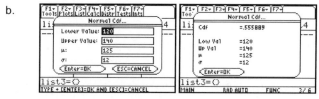

Answer: 0.556 · 100 = 55.6 %

c.

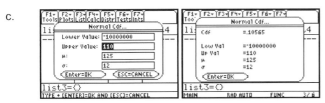

Answer: 0.106 · 100 = 10.6%

d.

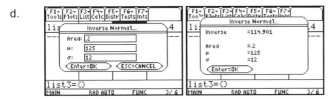

Answer: 114.9

Regression

Although regression is not part of the SAT math subject tests curriculum, it becomes handy in two particular cases:

1. Finding the equation of a line given two different points on it.

2. Finding the equation of a parabola given three different points on it.

Example: Find the equation of the line through the points (1, 3) and (2, –4)?

Solution:

We need to enter the x values to list1; the y values to list2, then perform linear regression (**linreg**) accessible through the **MATH Statistics Regression** submenu.

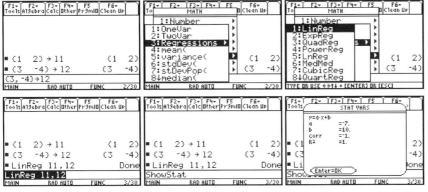

OR

We may perform the same steps using the **Statistics with List Editor App for the TI–89 Titanium** as follows:

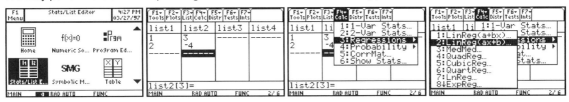

Answer: y = –7x + 10

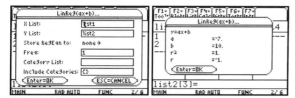

Example: Find the equation of the parabola through the points (1, 4), (0, 3), and (–1, 6)?

Solution:

We need to enter the x values to list1; the y values to list2, then perform quadratic regression (**quadreg**) accessible through the **MATH Statistics Regression** submenu.

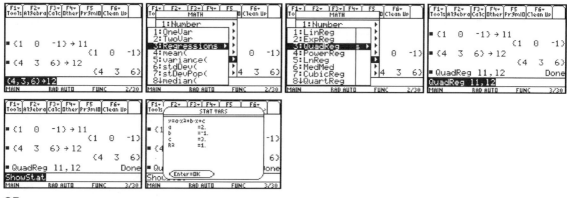

OR

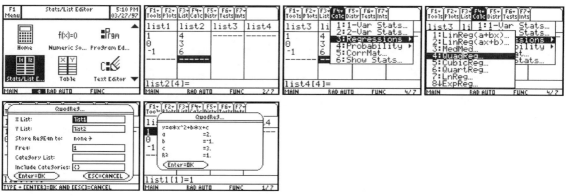

Answer: $y = 2x^2 - x + 3$

1.25 $\boxed{F_2}$ – ALGEBRA MENU

The $\boxed{F_2}$ **Algebra** menu is among the most helpful properties of TI-89. In this menu the **utilities solve(, factor(, expand(, zeros(, csolve(, cfactor(, and czeros(** are very useful.

Before we explore what each of these are useful for, we would like to give the following information on polynomials.

- Every polynomial with a degree of n has exactly n zeros. Some can be real, some can be complex, some can be positive, some can be negative, some can be integers or rational or irrational, some can be the same and some can be different. However the total number of zeros is always n.

- If P(x) is a real polynomial (a polynomial with real coefficient) then complex (non – real) zeros appear in conjugate pairs. If p + qi is a root so is p – qi or vice versa where i = $\sqrt{-1}$ and p and q are real numbers. Therefore a real polynomial has definitely an even number of complex zeros.

Working with Polynomials with TI–89

Illustrative example: P(x) = $x^5 + 3x^4 + 4x^3 + 8x^2 - 16$ is a polynomial function whose zeros are as follows:

$x_1 = x_2 = -2$; $x_3 = 1$; $x_4 = 2i$ and $x_5 = -2i$

Please note that –2 is a double zero, i.e. it has a multiplicity of 2; and the polynomial has two complex conjugate zeros since its coefficients are real.

- **solve(** will give the real zeros; and any repeated zeros will be listed only once.

    solve($x^5 + 3x^4 + 4x^3 + 8x^2 - 16 = 0$, x)

    x = –2 or x = 1

- **factor(** will give the real factors only.

    factor($x^5 + 3x^4 + 4x^3 + 8x^2 - 16$, x)

    $(x + 2)^2(x - 1)(x^2 + 4)$

    In an indirect way this utility gives the real zeros along with the multiplicity of each zero.

- **zeros(** will give the real zeros; and any repeated zeros will be listed only once.

    zeros($x^5 + 3x^4 + 4x^3 + 8x^2 - 16$, x)

    {–2, 1}

- **csolve(** will give all zeros; real or complex and any repeated zeros will be listed only once.

    solve($x^5 + 3x^4 + 4x^3 + 8x^2 - 16 = 0$, x)

    x = –2 or x = 1 or x = 2i or x = –2i

- **cfactor(** will give all factors real and complex.

    cfactor($x^5 + 3x^4 + 4x^3 + 8x^2 - 16$, x)

    $(x + 2)^2(x - 1)(x + 2i)(x - 2i)$

    In an indirect way this utility gives all zeros of a polynomial along with the multiplicity of each zero.

- **czeros(** will give all zeros, real and complex; and any repeated zeros will be listed only once.

    zeros($x^5 + 3x^4 + 4x^3 + 8x^2 - 16$, x)

    {–2, 1, –2i, 2i}

Solving Algebraic Equations:

Example: $5x^{4/3} = 2 \Rightarrow x = ?$

Solution:

Solve(5x^(4/3) = 2, x) ⊢ ENTER

0.503 or –0.503.

Example: $2x - \dfrac{5}{x} + 2 = 0 \Rightarrow x = ?$

Solution:

Solve(2x – 5/x + 2 = 0, x) ⊢ ENTER

x = –2.158 or x = 1.158

Example: $x^2 + 2x = x(x + 2) \Rightarrow x = ?$

Solution:

Solve(x^2 + 2x = x(x + 2), x) ⊟ ENTER

Result: True

Answer: All real numbers

Solving Absolute Value Equations:

Example: $|x - 3| + |2x + 1| = 6 \Rightarrow x = ?$

Solution:

Solve(abs(x – 3) + abs(2x + 1) = 6, x) ⊟ ENTER

–1.33 or 2

Example: $|4x + 6| = 3x + 4 \Rightarrow x = ?$

Solution:

Solve(abs(4x + 6) = 3x + 4, x) ⊟ ENTER

Result: False

Answer: No solution

Example: $|2x - 6| = 6 - 2x \Rightarrow x = ?$

Solution:

Solve(abs(4x + 6) = 3x + 4, x) ⊟ ENTER

Answer: x ≤ 3

Solving Exponential Equations:

Example: $2^{x + 3} = 3^x \Rightarrow x = ?$

Solution:

Solve(2^(x + 3) = 3^x, x) ⊟ ENTER

x = 5.129

Solving Logarithmic Equations:

Example: $\log_x 3 = \log_4 x \Rightarrow x = ?$

Solution:

solve(ln(3)/ln(x) = ln(x)/ln(4), x) ⊟ ENTER

x = 0.291 or x = 3.435

Solving a System of Non Linear Equations:

Example: SOLVING FOR NUMBERS

If $x - y = 2$ and $x^2 - y^2 = 6$ then x = ? and y = ?

Solution:

Solve(x – y = 2 and $x^2 - y^2 = 6$, {x, y}) ⊟ ENTER

x = 2.5 and y = 0.5

Example: SOLVING FOR LITERALS

$x - y = a$

$x^2 - y^2 = b$

x = ? and y = ?

Solution:

Solve($x - y = a$ and $x^2 - y^2 = b$, {x, y}) ⊟ ENTER

$x = \dfrac{a^2 + b}{2a}$ and $y = \dfrac{-a^2 + b}{2a}$

Solving a System of Linear Equations:

Example:

$x + 3y = 7$

$12x - 2y = 8$

x = ? and y = ?

Solution:

Solve(x + 3y = 7 and 12x − 2y = 8, {x, y}) ⊟ ENTER

x = 1 and y = 2

Example:

$x + y + z = 6$

$2x - y + 3z = 9$

$3x + y - 4z = -7$

x = ? y = ? and z = ?

Solution:

Solve(x + y + z = 6 and 2x − y + 3z = 9 and 3x + y − 4z = −7, {x, y, z}) ⊟ ENTER

x = 1 and y = 2 and z = 3

Solving Inverse Trigonometric Equations:

Example: Solve for x: $\cos^{-1}(2x - 2x^2) = \dfrac{2\pi}{3} \Rightarrow$ x = ?

Solution:

Angle Angle mode: Radians

Solve($\cos^{-1}(2x - 2x\text{\textasciicircum}2) = 2\pi/3$, x) ⊟ ENTER

x = −0.207 or x = 1.207

Example: $\sin^{-1}(x) = 3$ Arccosx $\Rightarrow$ x = ?

Solution:

Angle Angle mode: Radians

solve($\sin^{-1}(x) = 3\cos^{-1}(x)$, x) ⊟ ENTER

x = 0.92

What lies behind us and what lies before us are tiny matters compared to what lies within us.

Ralph Waldo EMERSON

CHAPTER 2.

GRAPHING WITH TI–89

Great spirits have always encountered violent opposition from mediocre minds.

Albert EINSTEIN

TI–89 family has many superior facilities compared to the TI–83/84 family with a primary difference; with TI–89 every mathematical expression must be correctly entered where every parenthesis will have to be closed unlike that in TI–83/84.

2.1 Mode Settings

The commonly used mode settings are:

- **Graph: FUNCTION, PARAMETRIC, POLAR**

- **Angle: RADIAN, DEGREE**

- **Complex Format: REAL, RECTANGULAR, POLAR;** if in the **RECTANGULAR** format, complex calculations can be carried out and the answers will be displayed in a + bi form; if in the **POLAR** format, complex calculations can be carried out and the answers will be displayed in $r \cdot e^{i\theta}$ form.

- **Exact/Approx: AUTO, EXACT, APPROXIMATE;** we suggest that this mode be left in the **APPROXIMATE** selection.

2.2 The Y = Editor

The graphs of functions etc. can be input using the Y = editor. The Y = editor can be accessed by pressing the $\boxed{F_1}$ key.

Mode setting	Variable to be used
Function	X
Parametric	T
Polar	θ

2.3 Graph Style Icons in the Y = Editor

The following table describes the graph styles available for function graphing. Use the styles to visually differentiate functions to be graphed together. For example, you can set Y_1 as a solid line, Y_2 as a dotted line, and Y_3 as a thick line as follows:

NAME	DESCRIPTION
Dot	A small dot represents each plotted point; this is the default in Dot mode. This is the style that must be used for plotting functions involving jump discontinuities such as the greatest integer function, i.e. int(x) so that false vertical lines will be eliminated while plotting the graphs.
Thick	A thick solid line connects plotted points.
Above	Shading covers the area above the graph. This is the style that must be used for plotting y > f(x) or y ≥ f(x) type of graphs.
Below	Shading covers the area below the graph. This is the style that must be used for plotting y < f(x) or y ≤ f(x) type of graphs.

The graph styles can be changed using the F_6 menu after the function is input.

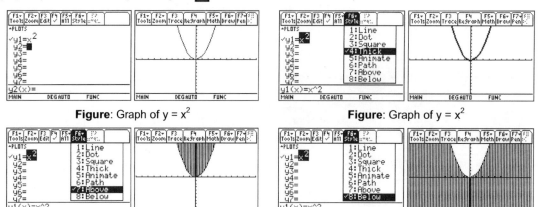

Figure: Graph of y = x^2 **Figure**: Graph of y = x^2

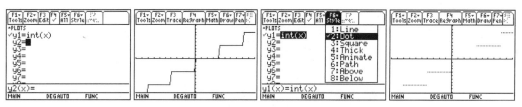

Figure: Graph of y > x^2 **Figure**: Graph of y < x^2

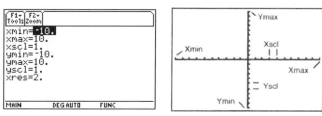

2.4 Graph Viewing Window Settings

The viewing window is the portion of the coordinate plane defined by **Xmin, Xmax, Ymin,** and **Ymax. Xscl** (X scale) defines the distance between tick marks on the x – axis. **Yscl** (Y scale) defines the distance between tick marks on the y – axis. To turn off tick marks, set **Xscl = 0** and **Yscl = 0.**

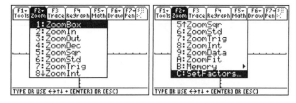

Viewing window settings can be accessed by using the ♦ F_2 key combination.

2.5 The ZOOM Menu

The **ZOOM** menu can be accessed by pressing the F_2 key after a function is graphed.

Commonly used **ZOOM** functions in the SAT II Math context are as follows:

Zoom Box	Draws a box to define the viewing window.
Zoom In	Magnifies the graph around the cursor.
Zoom Out	Views more of a graph around the cursor.
Zoom Sqr	Sets equal – size pixels on the X and Y axes.
Zoom Std	Sets the standard window variables.
Zoom Fit	Fits Ymin and Ymax between Xmin and Xmax.

2.6 The **F₅** – Math Menu

The **F₅** menu items that will be heavily used in the context of SAT II Math are **value**, **zero**, **minimum**, **maximum** and **intersection**.

Suppose we would like to find the zeros, the local maximum and the local minimum point of the following function. Suppose we would also like to find the intersection point(s) of this function with another function that will be given.

Firstly the function $y = x^3 - x^2 - 2x + \dfrac{1}{2}$ will be plotted and zoomed in once to get a clear viewing of the zeros, maximum and minimum point.

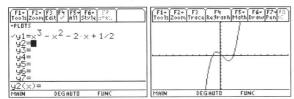

i. **F₅** value

The **value** facility will calculate the y–coordinate of a point whose x–coordinate that must be within the viewing window is to be entered by the user. The x–coordinate can be any value, positive, or negative within the viewing window and multiple y coordinates can be calculated one after another by selecting **F₅** value only once.

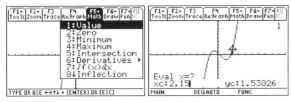

The x–coordinate to be entered can also be any correct mathematical expression that is within the viewing window. The expression will be calculated and converted to a decimal number that will be the corresponding x–coordinate and then the y–coordinate will be calculated similarly.

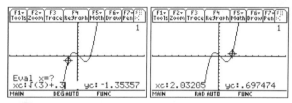

ii. F5 zero

The zeros of a function are the points, whose y – coordinates are zero. The F5 zero facility will enable the user to find such points that lie within the viewing window.

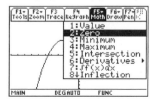

When F5 zero is selected, the user will be prompted to select the **Lower Bound**, and the **Upper Bound** of the zero that is to be found. Since zero is a point where the graph of the function "cuts" the x – axis, the graph has to have a sign change in the neighborhood of the zero. That is, in the neighborhood of the zero, it has to go **from negative (below the x – axis) to positive (above the x – axis) demonstrating an increasing function** or **from positive (above the x – axis) to negative (below the x – axis) demonstrating a decreasing function**.

So the graph will look like either one of the following in the neighborhood of the zero:

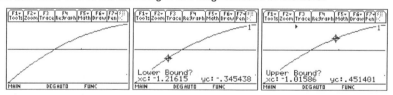

Figure Graph goes from negative (below the x – axis) to positive (above the x – axis):

Increasing behavior in the neighborhood of the zero.

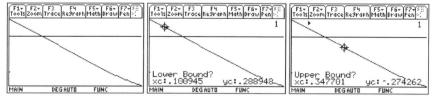

Figure Graph goes from positive (above the x – axis) to negative (below the x – axis):

Decreasing behavior in the neighborhood of the zero.

If the **graph** cuts the x – axis in an **increasing** fashion, the **Lower Bound** must be given **from below** the x – axis and the **Upper Bound** must be given **from above** the x – axis as is in the upper set of the preceding graphs. If the **graph** cuts the x – axis in a **decreasing** fashion, the **Lower Bound** must be given **from above** the x – axis and the **Upper Bound** must be given **from below** the x – axis as is in the lower set of the preceding graphs. If the Lower Bound and the Upper Bound are not entered correctly, an error message will appear on the screen. The Lower Bound and the Upper Bound can also be entered manually. In this case, the Lower Bound will be the x–coordinate of a point to the left of the zero and the Upper Bound will be the x–coordinate of a point to the right of the zero. This option is especially useful when the cursor does not appear on the screen or when the graph increases or decreases so steeply that the locations of the Lower Bound and the Upper Bound cannot be very easily seen.

If the graph of the function is tangent to the x – axis as shown in the following graphs, **F₅** **minimum** or **maximum** facilities must be used, that will be explained in the following sections.

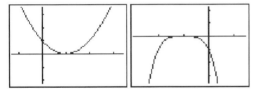

If the Lower Bound and the Upper Bound are not entered correctly, an error message will be displayed.

iii. **F₅** minimum

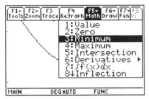

When **F₅** **minimum** is selected, the user will be prompted to select the **Lower Bound**, and the **Upper Bound** of the minimum that is to be found. The Lower Bound must be chosen as a point to the left of the crater of the minimum and the Upper Bound must be chosen as a point to the right of the crater of the minimum.

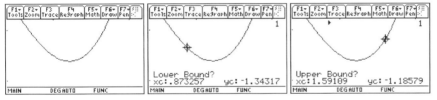

The Lower Bound and the Upper Bound can also be entered manually. Please note that if the Lower Bound and the Upper Bound are chosen both from the same side of the minimum, there will **NOT** be any error message, and the TI–89 will locate the point lower than the other one that is the point whose y–coordinate is smaller. An error message will come up when the Lower and the Upper Bound are selected from reverse sides.

iv. **F₅** maximum

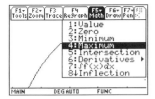

When **F₅** **maximum** is selected, the user will be prompted to select the **Lower Bound**, and the **Upper Bound** of the maximum that is to be found. The Lower Bound must be chosen as a point to the left of the crest of the maximum and the Upper Bound must be chosen as a point to the right of the crest of the maximum.

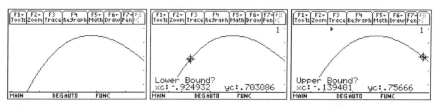

The Lower Bound and the Upper Bound can also be entered manually. Please note that if the Lower Bound and the Upper Bound are chosen both from the same side of the maximum, there will **NOT** be any error message, and the TI–89 will locate the point upper than the other one, that is the point whose y–coordinate is greater. The only error message will come up when the left and Upper Bound are selected from reverse sides.

v. F₅ intersection

The F₅ **intersection** facility is designed to find the intersection points of functions. In order to be able to use this facility there has to be at least two functions entered in the y – editor.

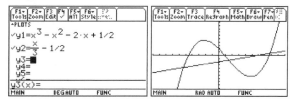

The usage of this facility is simpler than the other ones. The user is prompted to select the first curve and the second curve by pressing the ▼ and the ▲ keys and then guess the intersection point by moving the cursor to the location of the intersection point. When there are only two curves, there is no need to use the ▼ and the ▲ keys to select the curves the curves may be selected rapidly by pressing the enter key twice. The only task left in this case will be to give the lower bound and the upper bound of the point of intersection. Coming next is a demonstration of how to use this facility to find a desired intersection point. Please note that the only intersection points that can be found are the ones within the viewing window.

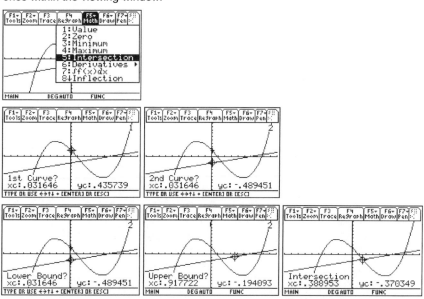

We have seen previously that it is possible to calculate the y–coordinate of a point on the function whose x–coordinate is given by using the F₅ **value** facility. The F₅ **intersection** facility enables us to find the x–coordinate of a point whose y–coordinate is given. If we would like to find the x coordinates of the points whose y coordinates are – 1/2 we would insert y = –1/2 for the second curve and find the intersection points using the $\boxed{F_5}$ **intersection** facility.

2.7 Table

When one or more functions are entered in the **Y = Editor**, TI–89 allows the user to construct a table of y values that correspond to the x values whose **starting value** and **increment size** are given by the user. The starting value is the **TblStart** variable and the increment is the **ΔTbl** variable in the **TBLSET**.

(Table Setup) Menu that can be accessed through the key combination of $\boxed{\blacklozenge}$ $\boxed{F_4}$.

The resulting table can be accessed through the key combination of $\boxed{\blacklozenge}$ $\boxed{F_5}$.

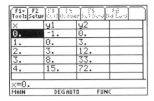

2.8 Graphing Piecewise Functions

Piecewise Functions are those that are not defined by a single unique formula. TI-89 allows the user to enter and plot such functions, via the **when(** function accessible through the **CATALOG**:

Let us consider the following examples:

Example: A piecewise function with two conditions; in this case we use a single **when(** function.

$$f(x) = \begin{cases} 9 - \dfrac{x^2}{5} & x \geq 2 \\ x - 1 & x < 2 \end{cases}$$

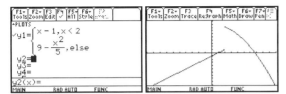

Example: A piecewise function with three conditions; in this case we use two **when(** functions nested within one another.

$$f(x) = \begin{cases} 2 & x \leq -2 \\ x^2 & -2 < x < 1 \\ -x + 3 & x \geq 1 \end{cases}$$

The above function must be entered and will be graphed as follows:

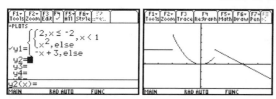

The required inequality signs are accessible through the **MATH** **Test** submenu:

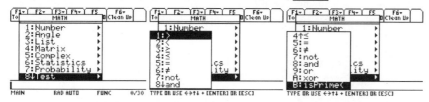

2.9 Composition of Functions – Operations and Transformations on Functions

Let us say that we are given two functions $f(x) = x^2$ and $g(x) = 1 - x$ and we would like to plot $(fog)(x) = f(g(x))$ and

$(gof)(x) = g(f(x))$.

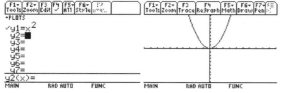

The following screen captures correspond to $(fog)(x) = (1 - x)^2$.

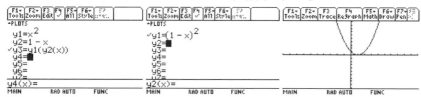

Please note that we have erased the check mark to the left of y1 and y2 in order to hide them on the display by

pressing the F4 key (which turns the check mak on and off).

The following screen captures correspond to $(gof)(x) = 1 - x^2$.

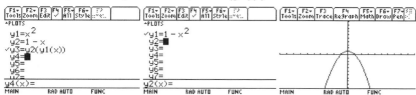

The following screen captures correspond to $(f + g)(x) = f(x) + g(x) = x^2 + 1 - x$.

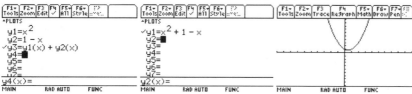

The following screen captures correspond to f(x − 1) + 1 = (x − 1)^2 + 1.

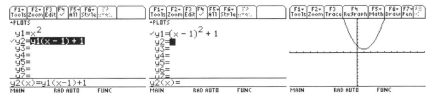

Parametric graphing allows the user to plot y versus x when the y and x variables are defined in terms of a **parameter "T"** which usually denotes the time variable (for example y and x can represent the y and x – coordinates that define the position of an object at time t). Settings must be changed to the **Parametric** mode so that the Y = Editor will enable that the relation between y and x be both defined in terms of the parameter **T**.

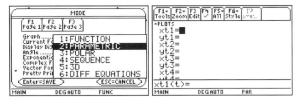

For example the following relation

x = 3cos(t)   y = 2sin(t)

It must be input as follows (t will be replaced by T)   and the output will be an ellipse.

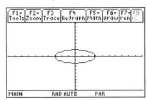

The important issue in the **Parametric** mode is the fact that the **T** variable in TI–89 is designed to represent the time variable **t** and therefore the default value for **tmin** in the window settings is 0 (zero) as time is supposed to be always nonnegative.

However, **T** does not necessarily have to denote time. For example the **Parametric** equation above could also be given as follows: x = 3cos(θ)   y = 2sin(θ) where **θ** is a parameter that does not represent time. On the other hand although the variable used may be t, it may still not represent time, either. In such cases where the free variable does not denote time, leaving **tmin** as 0 will result in an incorrect and misleading graph that will represent only a portion of the actual graph. Therefore when **T** is not given to represent time, **tmin** must be changed to **–tmax**: The default settings for **tmax** in **Radian** mode is 2π that appears as 6.28… and **tmin** must be set to –2π that will also appear as –6.28… after enter key is pressed.

It is also essential to be aware of the fact that the Zoom Std (Zoom Standard) action will reset Tmin back to 0. Therefore after Zoom Std is performed tmin must be changed to –tmax again when needed. Please also read section 2.9.

2.11 Polar Graphing

Polar graphing allows the user to plot **r** versus **θ** where **r** denotes **radius**, **θ** denotes **angle** and **(r, θ)** represents the **polar coordinates**. Settings must be changed to the **Pol**ar mode so that the Y = Editor will enable that **r** be defined in terms of the parameter **θ** that can be accessed by the key combination ◄ ^.

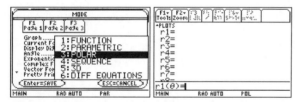

For example the input and output for the following relation r = 1 – 2cos(θ) will be as follows:

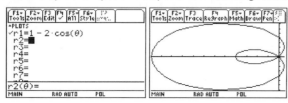

CHAPTER 3.

SUMMARY OF THE METHOD COVERED

IN THIS BOOK

We are what we repeatedly do. Excellence, therefore, is not an act but a habit.

ARISTOTLE

Summary of the Method Covered in this Book

Solving non–trigonometric equations

Please review section 1.25.

Solving trigonometric equations

When solving a trigonometric equation in the form **f(x) = g(x),** perform the following steps:

i. Write the equation in the form: **f(x) – g(x) = 0**.

ii. While writing the trigonometric expressions please observe the rules given in parts 1.17 and 1.18 that involve the trigonometric functions that are built in TI or otherwise.

iii. Plot the graph of **y = f(x) – g(x)**.

iv. Set the **angle mode to radians or degrees** depending on which angle measure is used in the question. If no degree signs (like in 90°) are used then the mode should be radians. However when exact values are required you may wish to solve the equation in degrees and convert the answer to radians using the following formula: $\dfrac{R}{\pi} = \dfrac{D}{180°}$. In such a case finding the answer in radians and then trying to find which answer choice matches this answer can also be an option; while doing so you may directly replace π with 180°

v. If x is limited to a certain interval then set **Xmin**; **Xmax** and **Xscl** accordingly. For example, if x is an acute angle and the angle mode is degrees, then **Xmin** must be set to 0°; **Xmax** must be set to 90° and **Xscl** must be set so that the grigding of the x – axis will be made properly In such a case **Xscl** being 30° would be fine. If x is an acute angle and the angle mode is radians, then **Xmin** must be set to 0; **Xmax** must be set to $\pi/2$ and **Xscl** may be set to 1.

vi. When only sines and cosines are involved, **ZoomFit** option may give a clearer graph. However, since only the x – intercepts are required, the window setting parameters **Ymin = –1** and **Ymax = 1** can give a clear view of the zeros.

vii. Find the x – intercepts using the **Calc Zero** of TI–89. However when the graph seems to be tangent to the x – axis at a certain point, you may use the **Calc Min** or **Calc Max** facilities but you should make sure that the y–coordinate of the minimum or maximum point is zero.

viii. Any value like **–6.61E –10** or **7.2E –11** can be interpreted as 0 as they mean **–6.6x10^{-10}** and **7.2x10^{-11}** respectively.

Solving inverse trigonometric equations

When solving an inverse trigonometric equation in the form **f(x) = g(x),** perform the following steps:

i. Write the equation in the form: **f(x) – g(x) = 0**.

ii. While writing the trigonometric expressions please observe the rules given in parts 1.17 and 1.18 that involve the trigonometric functions that are built in TI or otherwise.

iii. Plot the graph of **y = f(x) – g(x)**.

iv. Set the **angle mode to radians or degrees** depending on which angle measure is used in the question. If no degree signs (like in 90°) are used then the mode should be radians. However when exact values are required you may wish to solve the equation in degrees and convert the answer to radians using the formula: $\dfrac{R}{\pi} = \dfrac{D}{180°}$. In such a case finding the answer in radians and then trying to find which answer choice matches this answer can also be an option; while doing so you may directly replace π with $180°$

v.   Find the x – intercepts using the **Calc Zero** of TI–89. However when the graph seems to be tangent to the x – axis at a certain point, you may use the **Calc Min** or **Calc Max** facilities but you should make sure that the y–coordinate of the minimum or maximum point is zero.

vi.   Any value like **–6.61E –10** or **7.2E –11** can be interpreted as 0 as they mean **–6.6x10**$^{-10}$ and **7.2x10**$^{-11}$ respectively.

Solving non-trigonometric inequalities

When solving an inequality in the form **f(x) < g(x)**, or **f(x)≤g(x)**, or **f(x) > g(x)**, or **f(x)≥g(x)** perform the following steps:

i.   Write the inequality in the form: **f(x) – g(x) < 0** or **f(x) – g(x)≤0 or f(x) – g(x) > 0 or f(x) – g(x) ≥ 0.**

ii.   Plot the graph of **y = f(x) – g(x)**.

iii.   Find the x – intercepts using the **Calc Zero** of TI–89. However when the graph seems to be tangent to the x – axis at a certain point, you may use the **Calc Min** or **Calc Max** facilities but you should make sure that the y–coordinate of the minimum or maximum point is zero.

iv.   Any value like **–6.61E –10** or **7.2E –11** can be interpreted as 0 as they mean **–6.6x10**$^{-10}$ and **7.2x10**$^{-11}$ respectively.

v.   The solution of the inequality will be the set of values of x for which the graph of f(x) – g(x) lies below the x axis if the inequality is in one of the forms **f(x) – g(x) < 0** or **f(x) – g(x)≤0**. The solution of the inequality will be the set of values of x for which the graph of f(x) – g(x) lies above the x axis if the inequality is in one of the forms **f(x) – g(x) > 0** or **f(x) – g(x)≥0**. If $\leq$ or $\geq$ symbols are involved, then the x – intercepts are also in the solution set.

vi.   Please note that the x – values that correspond to asymptotes are never included in the solution set.

Solving trigonometric inequalities

When solving a trigonometric inequality in the form **f(x) < g(x)**, or **f(x)≤g(x)**, or **f(x) > g(x)**, or **f(x)≥g(x)** perform the following steps:

i.   Write the inequality in the form: **f(x) – g(x) < 0** or **f(x) – g(x)≤0 or f(x) – g(x) > 0 or f(x) – g(x)≥0.**

ii.   While writing the trigonometric expressions please observe the rules given in parts 1.17 and 1.18 that involve the trigonometric functions that are built in TI or otherwise.

iii.   Plot the graph of **y = f(x) – g(x)**.

iv.   Set the **angle mode to radians or degrees** depending on which angle measure is used in the question. If no degree signs (like in $90°$) are used then the mode should be radians. When exact values are required you may wish to solve the equation in degrees and convert the answer to radians using the formula $\dfrac{R}{\pi} = \dfrac{D}{180°}$. In such a case finding the answer in radians and then trying to find which answer choice matches this answer can also be an option; while doing so you may directly replace π with $180°$

v.   If x is limited to a certain interval then set **Xmin**; **Xmax** and **Xscl** accordingly. For example, if x is an acute angle and the angle mode is degrees, then **Xmin** must be set to $0°$; **Xmax** must be set to $90°$ and **Xscl** must be set so that the grigding of the x – axis will be made properly In such a case **Xscl** being 30° would be fine. If x is an acute angle and the angle mode is radians, then **Xmin** must be set to 0; **Xmax** must be set to $\pi/2$ and **Xscl** may be set to 1.

vi. When only sines and cosines are involved, **ZoomFit** option may give a clearer graph. However, since only the x – intercepts are required, the window setting parameters **Ymin = –1** and **Ymax = 1** can give a clear view of the zeros.

vii. Find the x – intercepts using the **Calc Zero** of TI–89. However when the graph seems to be tangent to the x – axis at a certain point, you may use the **Calc Min** or **Calc Max** facilities but you should make sure that the y–coordinate of the minimum or maximum point is zero.

viii. Any value like **–6.61E –10** or **7.2E –11** can be interpreted as 0 as they mean **–6.6x10^{-10}** and **7.2x10^{-11}** respectively.

ix. The solution of the inequality will be the set of values of x for which the graph of f(x) – g(x) lies below the x axis if the inequality is in one of the forms **f(x) – g(x) < 0** or **f(x) – g(x)≤0**. The solution of the inequality will be the set of values of x for which the graph of f(x) – g(x) lies above the x axis if the inequality is in one of the forms **f(x) – g(x) > 0** or **f(x) – g(x)≥0.** If $\leq$ or $\geq$ symbols are involved, then the x – intercepts are also in the solution set.

x. Please note that the x – values that correspond to asymptotes are never included in the solution set.

Finding maxima and minima

When solving for the maximum and/or minimum points of a function **f(x)** perform the following steps:

i. If x is limited to a certain interval then set **Xmin**; **Xmax** and **Xscl** accordingly, otherwise use Zstandard facility while graphing **y = f(x)**.

ii. Use the **Calc Min** or **Calc Max** facilities to find the minimum and maximum point(s). However if the minimum or maximum points are at one or both of the ends of the interval, then find these points by using the **Calc Value** facility; while doing so, use the x – coordinates of the endpoints of the interval.

iii. Any value like **–6.61E –10** or **7.2E –11** can be interpreted as 0 as they mean **–6.6x10^{-10}** and **7.2x10^{-11}** respectively.

Finding domains and ranges

When finding the domain and range of a function **f(x)**, graph the function and simply find the set of x values for which f(x) is plotted. You may perform the following steps:

i. If x is limited to a certain interval then set **Xmin**; **Xmax** and **Xscl** accordingly, otherwise use Zstandard facility while graphing **y = f(x)**.

ii. Use the **Calc Zero, Calc Value, Calc Min,** or **Calc Max** facilities to find the zeros, minima and maxima.

iii. When asymptotes or discontinuities are involved, you may use the **TBLSET** and **TABLE** facilities to find the set of x values for which f(x) is undefined or not continuous.

iv. Any value like **–6.61E –10** or **7.2E –11** can be interpreted as 0 as they mean **–6.6x10^{-10}** and **7.2x10^{-11}** respectively.

Exploring evenness and oddness

When finding whether a function **f(x)** is **even**, **odd** or **neither**, graph the function and simply check the symmetry.

i. If f(x) is symmetric in the y – axis, then it is even.

ii. If f(x) is symmetric in the origin, then it is odd.

---

iii.   If f(x) is not symmetric in the y – axis or the origin then it is neither even nor odd.

Graphs of trigonometric functions

(i)   Most of the time one or more of the following are required concerning the graphs of the trigonometric functions. In order to find them all it is usually enough to find two adjacent maxima and the minimum point in between.

Period = The x – distance between two identical points in a periodic function; for example two adjacent maxima, minima or zeros.

Frequency = 1/Period

Amplitude = (Ymax – Ymin)/2

Offset = (Ymax + Ymin)/2

Axis of wave equation: y = Offset

(ii)   **y – intercept** is the point whose x–coordinate is zero.

(iii)   Use the window, **Calc Min**, **Calc Max**, **Calc Value**, and **Calc Zero** facilities in order to perform the above calculations.

The greatest integer function

The greatest integer function f(x) = [x] = [|x|] means "The greatest integer less than or equal to x".

Mathematical definition for the greatest integer function is as follows:

f(x) = k if k ≤ x < k + 1 and k = integer ⟹ f(x) = [x]

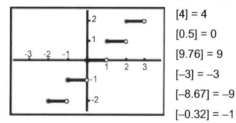

[4] = 4
[0.5] = 0
[9.76] = 9
[–3] = –3
[–8.67] = –9
[–0.32] = –1

TI Usage

y = int(x) and style must be set to dot as indicated in the following screen capture.

Parametric Graphing

Please review section 2.10.

Polar Graphing

Please review section 2.11.

Limits, continuity, horizontal and vertical asymptotes

(i)   For a function to have a limit for a given value of x = a, the right hand limit at a $^{+}$ and the left hand limit at a $^{-}$ must be the same and each limit must be equal to a real number L other than infinity.

Existence of Limit: If $\lim_{x \to a^{+}} f(x) = \lim_{x \to a^{-}} f(x) = L$ and $L \in R$ then $\lim_{x \to a} f(x) = L$

(ii)   Limit for a certain value of x or limit at infinity can be calculated by using the **STO**re facility of TI. What must be done is simply to store a value in x and calculate the value of the expression for this x – value.

(iii) ∞ can be replaced by 100, 000, 000, 000; and $-\infty$ can be replaced by -100, 000, 000, 000.

(iv)   Limit at a value of x other than $\pm\infty$ must be calculated as follows: If for example the limit at x = 3 will be calculated, 3.000000001 (which means the right hand limit at 3^{+}) must be stored in x and the expression must be evaluated; then 2.999999999 (which means the left hand limit at 3^{-}) must be stored in x and the expression must be evaluated again. If both limits are the same, say L, then the limit is equal to L, otherwise there is no limit.

For a function to be continuous at x = a, the right hand limit at a^{+} and the left hand limit at a^{-} must be the same and the limit must also be equal to the value of f(x) calculated at x = a.

If $\lim\limits_{x \to a^{+}} f(x) = \lim\limits_{x \to a^{-}} f(x) = f(a)$ then f(x) is continuous at x = a.

$f(x) = \dfrac{P(x)}{Q(x)}$ where P(x) and Q(x) are both polynomial functions.

(i)   **Zero:** If $P(x_o) = 0$ and $Q(x_o) \neq 0$ then f(x) has a zero at $x = x_o$.

(ii)   **Hole:** If $P(x_o) = 0$ and $Q(x_o) = 0$, and the multiplicity of x_o is the same in both polynomials, then f(x) has a hole at $x = x_o$

(iii)   **Vertical asymptote:** If $P(x_o) \neq 0$ but $Q(x_o) = 0$, then f(x) has a vertical asymptote at $x = x_o$

(iv)   **Horizontal asymptote:** If the limit of $\dfrac{P(x)}{Q(x)}$ equals b as x goes to $\pm\,\infty$ then y = b is the horizontal asymptote.

Complex numbers

(i)   Please review section 1.16.

(ii)   Calculator mode must be set to **a + bi** where i is the imaginary number that has the following properties: $i^2 = -1$ and $i = \sqrt{-1}$. The required functions can be found at the **MATH Complex** menu:

(iii)   **abs**$(a + bi) = \sqrt{a^2 + b^2}$; **real**(a + bi) = a; **imag**(a + bi) = b; **conj**(a + bi) = a – bi.

(iv)   cis(x) = cos(x) + i.sin(x)

(v) e^{ix} = cos(x) + i.sin(x)

Permutations and combinations

Please review section 1.21. and note the following: n! = n.(n – 1).(n – 2).(n – 3)...3.2.1

P(n, r): Number of permutations of r elements chosen from n elements; P(n, r) = $\dfrac{n!}{(n-r)!}$ and

C(n, r): Number of combinations of r elements chosen from n elements; C(n, r) = $\dfrac{n!}{(n-r)!.r!}$

where $r \leq n$. The required functions can be found at the **MATH Probability** menu.

<u>Important Note:</u>

Graphing approaches must be used when dealing with the following:

- Trigonometric Equations
- Polynomial, Algebraic and Absolute Value Inequalities
- Trigonometric Inequalities
- Maxima and Minima
- Domains and Ranges
- Evenness and Oddness
- Parametric Graphing
- Polar Graphing
- Graphs of Trigonometric Functions
    - Period
    - Frequency
    - Amplitude
    - Offset
    - Axis of wave equation
- Miscellaneous Graphs
- Greatest Integer Function
- Horizontal and Vertical Asymptotes

CHAPTER 4.

SAMPLE SAT 2 MATH SUBJECT TEST

PROBLEMS FULLY SOLVED WITH TI–89

Experience is a brutal teacher, but you learn. My God, do you learn.

C.S. LEWIS

1. $P(x) = 3x^3 - 5x^2 + 6x - 3$

   The zero of the above polynomial lies between two consecutive integers. What are these integers?

   Solution:

   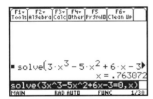

   Answer: Between 0 and 1

2. $y = 3x^2 - 4x - 5$

   What is the positive zero of the above function correct to the nearest hundredth?

   Solution:

   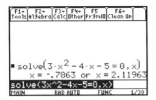

   Answer: 2.12

3. Is $x - 99$ a factor of the following polynomial?

   $P(x) = 2x^4 - 200x^3 + 194x^2 + 400x - 300$

   Solution:

   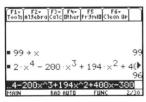

   Answer: NO because P(99) is not zero.

4. Find all real zeros of the following polynomial:

   $P(x) = 2x^6 - 2x^5 - 8x^4 - 2x^3 + 10x^2 + 16x + 8$

   Solution:

   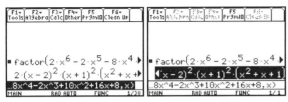

   Answer: Real zeros are −1 and 2 both of which are double.

5. What is the least positive integer greater than the zero of the following polynomial?

$$P(x) = -\frac{3}{2}x^3 - x^2 - 2x + 3$$

Solution:

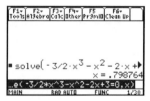

Answer: 1

6. What are the real roots of the following function?

$$f(x) = -2x^4 - 4x^3 + 6x^2 - 4x + 7$$

Solution:

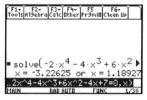

Answer: −3.226 and 1.189

7. $P(x) = 3x^4 - x^3 + 2x^2 + 5x - 1$

    How many positive and negative real zeros does the above polynomial have?

Solution:

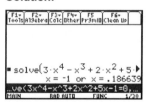

Answer: 1 positive and 1 negative real zero.

8. $x^2 + x + 2 = 0$

    What is the nature of the roots of the above equation?

Solution:

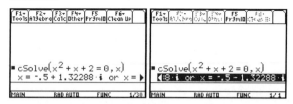

Answer: No real zeros, two complex conjugate zeros.

9. $P(x) = 2x^3 + x^2 + 3x - 5$

How many positive and negative real zeros does the above polynomial have?

Solution:

Answer: 1 positive real zero only.

10.   Find the positive rational root of the following equation:

$2x^3 - 5x^2 + 14\,x = 35$

Solution:

Answer: 2.5 or 5/2

11.   What is the absolute difference between the zeros of the following function?

$f(x) = 7x^2 + 11.5\,x - 25$

Solution:

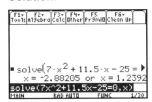

Answer: $1.239 - (-2.882) = 4.121$

12.   What is the sum of the zeros of the following parabola?

$y = 3x^2 - 7x - 5$

Solution:

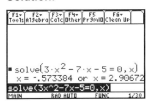

Answer: $2.907 + (-0.573) = 2.33$

13. What are the zeros of $y = 3x^2 + x - 4$?

Solution:

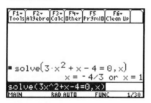

Answer: 1 and −1.333

14. $f(x) = 6x^2 + 12x - 3$; $f(q) = 0 \Rightarrow$ What is one value of q?

Solution:

Answer: −2.225 or 0.225.

15. Find the sum of the roots of $6x^3 + 8x^2 - 8x = 0$

Solution:

```
F1▼  F2▼  F3▼ F4▼  F5   F6▼
Tools Algebra Calc Other PrgmIO Clean Up

■ cZeros(6·x³ + 8·x² − 8·x, x)
           {-2.    0    .666667}
cZeros(6x^3+8x^2-8x,x)
MAIN      RAD APPROX  FUNC    1/30
```

Answer: −2 + 0 + .667 = −1.333

16. $P(x) = 2x^2 + 3x + 1$ and $P(a) = 7 \Rightarrow a = ?$

Solution:

```
F1▼  F2▼  F3▼ F4▼  F5   F6▼
Tools Algebra Calc Other PrgmIO Clean Up

■ solve(2·x² + 3·x + 1 = 7, x)
     x = -2.63746 or x = 1.13746
solve(2x^2+3x+1=7,x)
MAIN      RAD APPROX  FUNC    1/30
```

Answer: −2.637 or 1.137

17. What is the product of the roots of the following equation $(x - \sqrt{3})(x^2 - ex - \pi) = 0$?

Solution:

```
F1▼  F2▼  F3▼ F4▼  F5   F6▼
Tools Algebra Calc Other PrgmIO Clean Up

■ solve((x − √3)·(x² − e¹·x − ▶
     x = -.874434 or x = 1.7320▶
...3))*(x^2-e^(1)*x-π)=0,x)
MAIN      RAD APPROX  FUNC    1/30
```

Answer: − 0.87 · 1.73 · 3.59 = −5.44

18. $f(x) = 5x^2 - 7$

Find sum of the zeros of $f(x)$.

Solution:

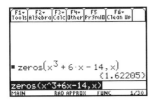

Answer: $-1.18 + 1.18 = 0$

19. $P(x) = x^3 + 6x - 14$ has a zero between which two consecutive integers?

Solution:

Answer: Between 1 and 2.

20. $f(x) = x^2 - 9$ and $(f \circ f)(x) = 0 \Rightarrow$ What are the real values of x?

Solution:

$(f \circ f)(x) = (x^2 - 9)^2 - 9$

Answer: $-2.449, 2.449, -3.464$ or 3.464

21. $2x^4 + 3x^3 + 2x - 1 = 0$; Find nature of the roots.

Solution:

Answer: 1 positive real, 1 negative real and two complex conjugate roots.

22. Is 3x + 1 a factor of $2x^3 + 4x^2 - 4x - 3$?

Solution:

If 3x + 1 is a factor then –1/3 must be a zero of the polynomial.

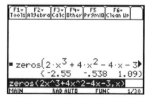

Answer: No

23. What is the remainder when $3x^4 + 8x^3 + 9x^2 - 3x - 4$ is divided by x + 1?

Solution:

Answer: 3

24. Find the number of positive real zeros of the following equation: $x^4 + 2x^3 - 4x^2 - 5x = 0$

Solution:

Answer: 1

25. Find product of the real roots of the following equation: $x^4 - 3x^3 - 72x^2 - 3x - 18 = 0$.

Solution:

$x^4 - 3x^3 - 72x^2 - 3x - 18 = 0$

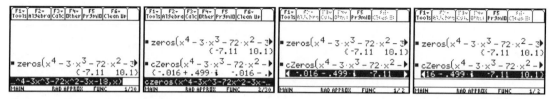

Answer: −7.11 x 10.14 = −72.09

26. $f(x) = 3x^2 + 8x - 6$; What is the negative value of $f^{-1}(0)$

Solution:

$f^{-1}(0) = x \Rightarrow f(x) = 0$; therefore $3x^2 + 8x - 6 = 0$

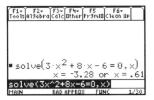

Answer: −3.28

1.

$f(x) = \sqrt{3x + 4}$ and $g(x) = x^3$; If is given what $(fog)(x) = (gof)(x)$, then what is x?

Solution:

$(fog)(x) = \sqrt{3x^3 + 4}$ and $(gof)(x) = (\sqrt{3x + 4})^3$

$\sqrt{3x^3 + 4} = (\sqrt{3x + 4})^3$

Answer: −1

2.

$f(x) = \sqrt{-x^3 + 4x}$ and $g(x) = 4x$; What is the sum of the roots of the equation $f(x) = g(x)$?

Solution:

$\sqrt{-x^3 + 4x} = 4x$

Answer: 0.246

3.

$a \# b = a^b - b^a$; If $3 \# k = k \# 2$ then k = ?

Solution:

$3^k - k^3 = k^2 - 2^k$

Answer: 2.294 or 3.228

4.

$5x^{4/3} = 2 \Rightarrow x = ?$

Solution:

$5x^{4/3} = 2$

Answer: 0.503 or −0.503.

5. Find sum of the roots of: $2x - \dfrac{5}{x} + 2 = 0$

Solution:

Answer: $-2.158 + 1.158 = -1$

1. $|3x - 1| = 4x + 6$

   How many numbers are there in the solution set of the above equation?

   Solution:

   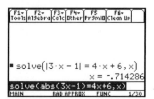

   Answer: 1

2. $|x - 3| + |2x + 1| = 6 \Rightarrow x = ?$

   Solution:

   $|x - 3| + |2x + 1| = 6$

   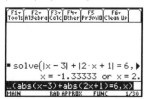

   Answer: $x = -1.33$ or 2

3. $|3x - 5| = 4 \Rightarrow x = ?$

   Solution:

   $|3x - 5| = 4$

   Answer: $x = 0.33$ or 3

4. $|4x + 6| = 3x + 4 \Rightarrow x = ?$

   Solution:

   Answer: No solution

5. $\dfrac{|x-3|}{x} = 4 \Rightarrow x = ?$

Solution:

$\dfrac{|x-3|}{x} = 4$

Answer: 0.6

1. $\log_4 x \cdot \log_5 6 = 7 \Rightarrow x = ?$

   Solution:

   $\log_4 x \cdot \log_5 6 = 7$

   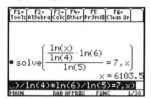

   Answer: 6103.5

2. $A = e^{Bt}$

   $A = 1000, \; T = 4, \; B = ?$

   Solution:

   $1000 = e^{B*4}$

   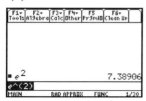

   Answer: 1.73

3. $f(x) = \exp(x)$; (please note that $\exp(x)$ and e^x have the same meaning). If $h(x) = f(-x) + f^{-1}(-x)$ then $h(-2) = ?$

   Solution:

   $h(-2) = f(2) + f^{-1}(2)$

   $f(2) = e^2 = 7.389$

   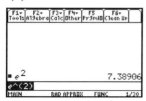

   $f^{-1}(2) = x \Rightarrow f(x) = e^x = 2$

   Answer: $7.389 + 0.693 = 8.082$

4. If $\log x = \dfrac{3}{4}$ then $\log(1000x^2) = ?$

    Solution:

    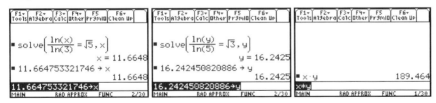

F1▼	F2▼	F3▼	F4▼	F5	F6▼

    ■ solve(log(x) = 3/4, x)
    $\qquad\qquad x = 5.62341$
    ■ 5.6234132519039 → x
    $\qquad\qquad\qquad 5.62341$
    ■ log(1000·x²)
    $\qquad\qquad\qquad 4.5$

    log(1000*x^2)

    MAIN   RAD APPROX   FUNC   3/30

    Answer: 4.5

5. $\log_3 2 = x \cdot \log_6 5 \Rightarrow x = ?$

    Solution:

F1▼	F2▼	F3▼	F4▼	F5	F6▼
Tools	Algebra	Calc	Other	PrgmIO	Clean Up

    ■ solve$\left(\dfrac{\ln(2)}{\ln(3)} = \dfrac{x \cdot \ln(5)}{\ln(6)}, x\right)$
    $\qquad\qquad x = .702403$

    ...)/ln(3)=x*ln(5)/ln(6),x)

    MAIN   RAD APPROX   FUNC   1/30

    Answer: 0.702

6. $\left.\begin{array}{l} \log_3 x = \sqrt{5} \\ \log_5 y = \sqrt{3} \end{array}\right\}$ $xy = ?$

    Solution:

    $\log_3 x = \sqrt{5}$ so $\log_3 x - \sqrt{5} = 0$

F1▼ F2▼ F3▼ F4▼ F5 F6▼	F1▼ F2▼ F3▼ F4▼ F5 F6▼	F1▼ F2▼ F3▼ F4▼ F5 F6▼
■ solve$\left(\dfrac{\ln(x)}{\ln(3)} = \sqrt{5}, x\right)$ $\;x = 11.6648$ ■ 11.664753321746 → x 11.6648	■ solve$\left(\dfrac{\ln(y)}{\ln(5)} = \sqrt{3}, y\right)$ $\;y = 16.2425$ ■ 16.242450820886 → y 16.2425	■ x·y $\qquad 189.464$
11.664753321746→x	16.242450820886→y	x*y
MAIN RAD APPROX FUNC 2/30	MAIN RAD APPROX FUNC 2/30	MAIN RAD APPROX FUNC 1/30

    Answer: 11.66 * 16.24 = 189.36

7. $2^{x+3} = 3^x \Rightarrow x = ?$

    Solution:

    $2^{x+3} = 3^x$

F1▼	F2▼	F3▼	F4▼	F5	F6▼
Tools	Algebra	Calc	Other	PrgmIO	Clean Up

    ■ solve$\left(2^{x+3} = 3^x, x\right)$
    $\qquad\qquad x = 5.12853$

    solve(2^(x+3)=3^x,x)

    MAIN   RAD APPROX   FUNC   1/30

    Answer: 5.129

---

8. $\log_x 3 = \log_4 x \Rightarrow$ What is the sum of the roots of this equation?

Solution:

$\log_x 3 = \log_4 x$

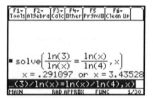

Answer: 0.291 + 3.435 = 3.726

9. $f(x) = 3.5^x + 1; f^{-1}(10) = ?$

Solution:

$f^{-1}(10) = x \Rightarrow f(x) = 10$; therefore $3.5^x + 1 = 10$

Answer: 1.754

10. $3.281^x = 4.789^y \Rightarrow \dfrac{x}{y} = ?$

Solution:

If $y = 1$ then $\dfrac{x}{y} = x \Rightarrow 3.281^x = 4.789^1 = 4.789$

Answer: 1.318

1. $\begin{aligned} x + 3y &= 7 \\ 12x - 2y &= 8 \end{aligned}\biggr\} \dfrac{x}{y} = ?$

    Solution:

    Answer: 1/2

2. Find the determinant and inverse of the matrix $\begin{bmatrix} 1 & 3 & -1 \\ -2 & 4 & 1 \\ 0 & 0 & 2 \end{bmatrix}$

    Solution:

    Answer: $|A| = 20$ and $A^{-1} = \begin{bmatrix} 0.4 & -0.3 & 0.35 \\ 0.2 & 0.1 & 0.05 \\ 0 & 0 & 0.5 \end{bmatrix}$

3. $\begin{aligned} x + y + z &= 6 \\ 2x - y + 3z &= 9 \\ 3x + y - 4z &= -7 \end{aligned}\Biggr\} x^2 + y^2 + z^2 = ?$

    Solution:

    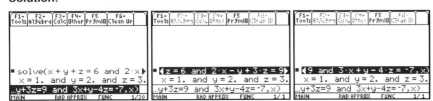

    Answer: $1^2 + 2^2 + 3^2 = 1 + 4 + 9 = 14$

4. If $A = \begin{bmatrix} 2 & 3 \\ -1 & 5 \end{bmatrix}$, $B = \begin{bmatrix} 0 & -2 \\ -3 & 5 \end{bmatrix}$, Find (i)A + B; (ii) 3A − 2B; (iii) AB; (iv) BA

    Solution:

    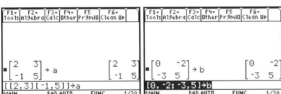

(i)   (ii)   (iii)   (iv)

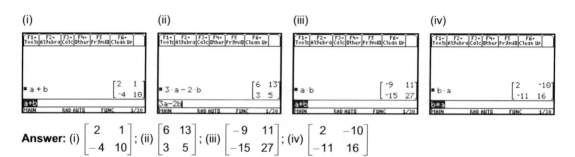

Answer: (i) $\begin{bmatrix} 2 & 1 \\ -4 & 10 \end{bmatrix}$; (ii) $\begin{bmatrix} 6 & 13 \\ 3 & 5 \end{bmatrix}$; (iii) $\begin{bmatrix} -9 & 11 \\ -15 & 27 \end{bmatrix}$; (iv) $\begin{bmatrix} 2 & -10 \\ -11 & 16 \end{bmatrix}$

4.6 Trigonometric Equations

1. How many solutions does the equation $\sec^2 x - \dfrac{\sin x}{\cos x} = 1$ have between 0° and 360°?

Solution:

Angle mode: Degrees

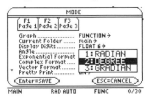

$$\sec^2 x - \frac{\sin x}{\cos x} - 1 = 0$$

Answer: The graph intersects with the x – axis 5 times in the given interval therefore there are 5 solutions.

2. $\cos(33°) = \tan x° \Rightarrow x = ?$ (x is an acute angle)

Solution:

Angle mode: Degrees

or

$$\cos(33°) - \tan x° = 0$$

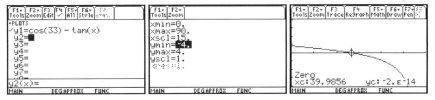

Answer: 39.99°

3. $0 < x < \dfrac{\pi}{4}$ and $\tan(4x) = 3$. What is x and what is tanx?

Solution:

Angle mode: Radians

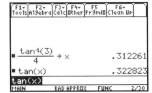

$\tan(4x) - 3 = 0$

Answer: $x = 0.312$ and $\tan x = 0.323$

4. $\sin(120° - n) = \sin 50°$ and n is an acute angle $\Rightarrow$ n = ?

Solution:

Angle mode: Degrees

$\sin(120° - n) - \sin 50° = 0$

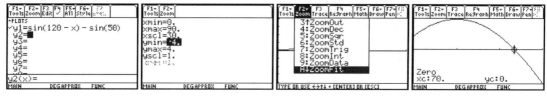

Answer: 70°

What is the sum of the two least positive solutions of the equation $\sin(10x) = -\cos(10x)$?

Solution:

Angle mode: Radians

$\sin(10x) = -\cos(10x) \Rightarrow \sin(10x) + \cos(10x) = 0$

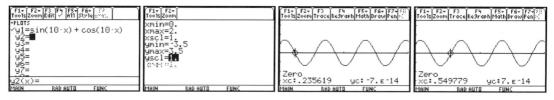

Answer: $0.24 + 0.55 = 0.79$

5. $\cos(2x) = 2\sin(90° - x)$. What are all possible values of x between 0° & 360°?

Solution:

Angle mode: Degrees

$\cos(2x) = 2\sin(90° - x) \Rightarrow \cos(2x) - 2\sin(90° - x) = 0$

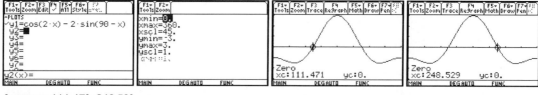

Answer: 111.47°, 248.53°

---

6. $\dfrac{1}{4}\sin^2(2x) + \sin^2(x) + \cos^4(x) = 1$

    If x is positive and less than 2π, how many different values can x have?

    Solution:

    Angle mode: Radians

    $\dfrac{1}{4}\sin^2(2x) + \sin^2(x) + \cos^4(x) - 1 = 0$

    Answer: x has infinitely many values between $(0, 2\pi)$

7. If $\dfrac{1}{\cot(5x)} = -2$ then what is the smallest positive value for x?

    Solution:

    Angle mode: Radians

    $\dfrac{1}{\cot(5x)} = -2 \ \Rightarrow \ \dfrac{1}{\cot(5x)} + 2 = 0$

    Answer: 0.41

8. $\dfrac{8\sin(2\theta)}{1-\cos(2\theta)} = \dfrac{4}{3}$ and θ is between 0° and 180°. What is θ?

    Solution:

    Angle mode: Degrees

    $\dfrac{8\sin(2\theta)}{1-\cos(2\theta)} = \dfrac{4}{3} \Rightarrow \dfrac{8\sin(2\theta)}{1-\cos(2\theta)} - \dfrac{4}{3} = 0$

    Answer: 80.53

9. $\dfrac{\sin x + \cos 36°}{\cos\dfrac{4\pi}{3} - \sin(-90°)} = 0$ and x is between 90° and 270° $\Rightarrow$ x = ?

Solution:

Angle mode: Degrees

Answer: 234°

10. $\dfrac{\sin\theta}{\cos\theta - 1} = -\sqrt{3}$ $\Rightarrow$ If θ is an acute angle, θ = ?

Solution:

Angle mode: Radians

$$\dfrac{\sin\theta}{\cos\theta - 1} + \sqrt{3} = 0$$

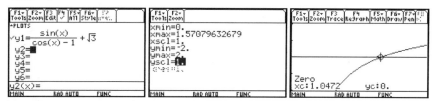

Answer: 1.05

11. $2\sin x + \cos(2x) = 2\sin^2 x - 1$ and $0 \le x < 2\pi \Rightarrow$ x = ?

Solution:

Angle mode: Radians

$2\sin x + \cos(2x) = 2\sin^2 x - 1 \Rightarrow 2\sin x + \cos(2x) - 2\sin^2 x + 1 = 0$

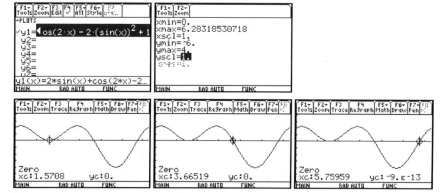

Answer: 1.57, 3.67, 5.76

12. $\cos(130° - 2x) = \sin(70° - 3x)$ and x is an acute angle. What is x?

Solution:

Angle mode: Degrees

$\cos(130° - 2x) = \sin(70° - 3x) \Rightarrow \cos(130° - 2x) - \sin(70° - 3x) = 0$

Answer: 22°

13. x is in quadrant 3 and $\cot(120° - x) = \dfrac{1}{\tan x} \Rightarrow x = ?$

Solution:

Angle mode: Degrees

$$\cot(120° - x) - \dfrac{1}{\tan x} = 0$$

Answer: 240°

14. $\left.\begin{array}{l} \dfrac{\sin(2\theta)}{2} = \dfrac{1}{4} \\[2mm] 0° \le \theta < 360° \end{array}\right\}$ What is θ?

Solution:

Angle mode: Degrees

$$\dfrac{\sin(2\theta)}{2} - \dfrac{1}{4} = 0$$

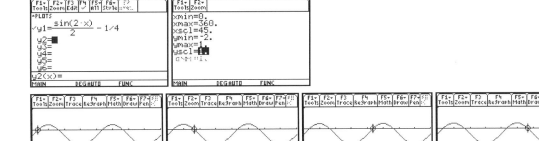

Answer: 15°, 75°, 195°, 255°

15. $$\left.\begin{array}{l} \sec\theta\cdot\csc\theta = 4 \\ 0° \le \theta < 360° \end{array}\right\} \theta = ?$$

Solution:

Angle mode: Degrees

$\sec\theta\cdot\csc\theta - 4 = 0$

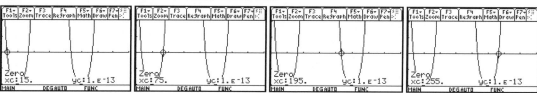

Answer: 15°, 75°, 195°, 255°

16. $$\left.\begin{array}{l} 0° \le x < 90° \\ \tan(4x) = 1 \end{array}\right\} x = ?$$

Solution:

Angle mode: Degrees

$\tan(4x) - 1 = 0$

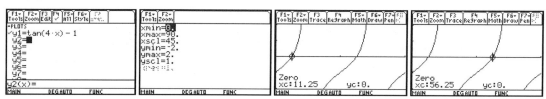

Answer: 11.25° and 56.25°

17. $\tan(6x) = \sqrt{3}$ and x is an acute angle $\Rightarrow$ x = ?

Solution:

Angle mode: Radians

$\tan(6x) - \sqrt{3} = 0$

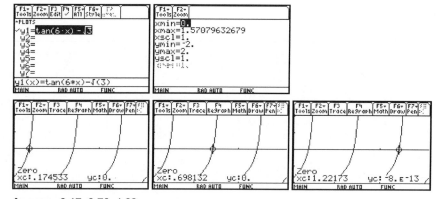

Answer: 0.17, 0.70, 1.22

18. $\left.\begin{array}{r}\dfrac{\sqrt{3}}{2}\cos x + \dfrac{1}{2}\sin x = 1 \\ 0 \le x < 2\pi\end{array}\right\} \Rightarrow x = ?$

Solution:

Angle mode: Radians

$$\dfrac{\sqrt{3}}{2}\cos x + \dfrac{1}{2}\sin x - 1 = 0$$

Answer: 0.52

19. $2\sin^2 x = 3(1 + \cos x) - \dfrac{1}{2}$ and x is in 3rd quadrant. What is x in radians?

Solution:

Angle mode: Radians

$$2\sin^2 x - 3(1 + \cos x) + \dfrac{1}{2} = 0$$

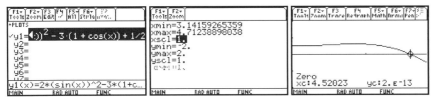

Answer: 4.52

20. $\cos x \cdot \cos 45° - \sin x \cdot \sin 45° = -1$ and x is an obtuse angle $\Rightarrow x = ?$

Solution:

Angle mode: Degrees

$$\cos x \cdot \cos 45° - \sin x \cdot \sin 45° + 1 = 0$$

Answer: 135°

21. $$\left.\begin{array}{l} \sin x \sec x = \sqrt{3} \\ 0 \le x < 2\pi \end{array}\right\} \Rightarrow x = ?$$

Solution:

Angle mode: Radians

$$\sin x \sec x - \sqrt{3} = 0$$

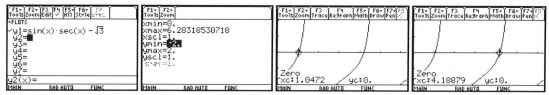

Answer: 1.05, 4.19

23. $\tan(-30^\circ) = -\cot x \Rightarrow x = ?$ (x is in 3rd quadrant)

Solution:

Angle mode: Degrees

$\tan(-30^\circ) + \cot x = 0$

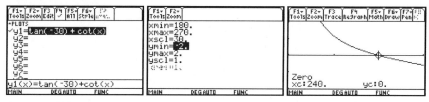

Answer: 240

4.7 Inverse Trigonometric Equations

1. Solve for x: $\cos^{-1}(2x - 2x^2) = \dfrac{2\pi}{3}$

    Solution:

    Angle mode: Radians

    $$\cos^{-1}(2x - 2x^2) - \frac{2\pi}{3} = 0$$

    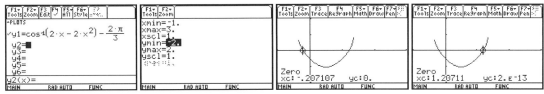

    Answer: −0.207 or 1.207

2. $\sin^{-1}(x) = 3 \, \text{Arccos} x \Rightarrow x = ?$

    Solution:

    Angle mode: Radians

    $$\sin^{-1}(x) - 3\,\text{Arccos} x = 0$$

    Answer: 0.92

3. Find B in degrees using the following system of equations.

    $$\left. \begin{aligned} A &= \text{Arctan}\left(\frac{-5}{12}\right) \\ A + B &= 300° \end{aligned} \right\}$$

    Solution:

    Angle mode: Degrees

    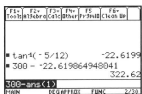

    Answer: 322.62°

4.8 Polynomial, Algebraic and Absolute Value Inequalities

Find the solution sets of the following inequalities:

1.　　$x^2 - 8x + 7 < 0$

Solution:

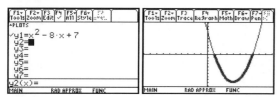

Answer: $(1, 7)$

2.　　$\dfrac{x}{x - 3} > 4$

Solution:

$$\dfrac{x}{x - 3} - 4 > 0$$

Answer: $(3, 4)$

3.　　$\dfrac{|x - 2|}{x} > 3$

Solution:

$$\dfrac{|x - 2|}{x} - 3 > 0$$

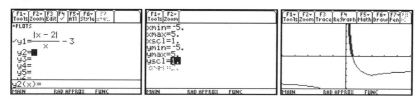

Answer: $(0, 0.5)$

4.　　$f(x) = x + \sqrt{2x + 1}$ and $f(x) \le 4$.

Solution:

$$x + \sqrt{2x + 1} - 4 \le 0$$

Answer: [−0.5, 1.84]

5.   x(x − 1)(x + 2)(x − 3) < 0

Solution:

Answer: (−2, 0) or (1, 3)

6.   x(x − 2)(x + 1) > 0

Solution:

Answer: (−1, 0) or (2, ∞)

7.   x²(x − 2)(x + 1) ≥ 0

Solution:

Answer: (−∞, −1] or {0} or [2, ∞)

8. $\dfrac{x + 2}{x} < 4$

Solution:

$$\frac{x + 2}{x} - 4 < 0$$

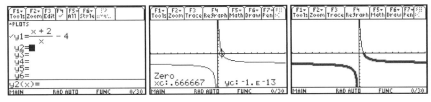

Answer: (−∞, 0) or (0.67, ∞)

9. $4x^2 - x < 3$

Solution:

$4x^2 - x - 3 < 0$

Answer: $(-0.75, 1)$

10. $\dfrac{(x+1)^2}{x^3} > 0$

Solution:

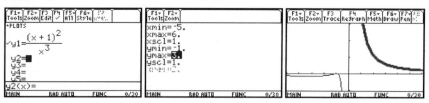

Answer: $(0, \infty)$

11. $|2x + 5| \geq 3$

Solution:

$|2x + 5| - 3 \geq 0$

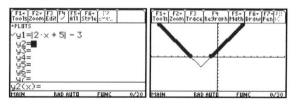

Answer: $(-\infty, -4]$ or $[-1, \infty)$

12. $|x - 2| \leq 1$

Solution:

$|x - 2| - 1 \leq 0$

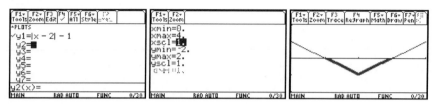

Answer: $[1, 3]$

13. $x^2 + 12 < 7x$

Solution:

$x^2 - 7x + 12 < 0$

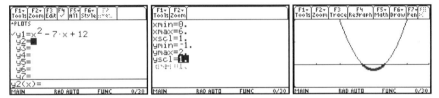

Answer: (3, 4)

14.   In which quadrants are the points that satisfy the following system of inequalities?

$y < -(x - 2)^2 - 1$

$y \geq 2x - 7$

Solution:

Answer: 3rd and 4th quadrants.

1. What is the solution set of the inequality given by x < cosx;?

   Solution:

   Angle mode: Radians

   $x - \cos x < 0$

   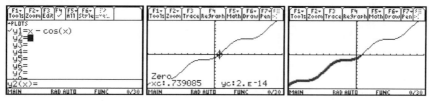

   Answer: $(-\infty, 0.74)$

2. $\sin(2x) > \sin x$

   Find the set of values of x that satisfy the above inequality in the interval $0 < x < 2\pi$.

   Solution:

   Angle mode: Radians

   $\sin(2x) - \sin x > 0$

   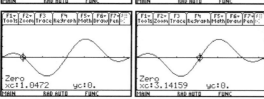

   Answer: (0, 1.05) or (3.14, 5.24)

3. If x is between 0 and 2π, what will be the set of x values for which sinx < cosx?

   Solution:

   Angle mode: Radians

   $\sin x - \cos x < 0$

   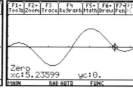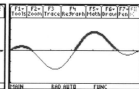

   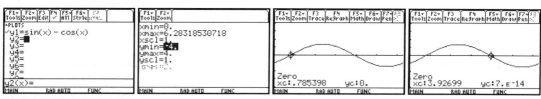

   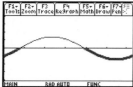

   Answer: (0, 0.79) or (3.93, 2π)

4. $\cos(2x) \geq \cos x$

Find the set of values of x that satisfy the above inequality in the interval $0 \leq x \leq 360°$.

Solution:

Angle mode: Degrees

$\cos(2x) - \cos x \geq 0$

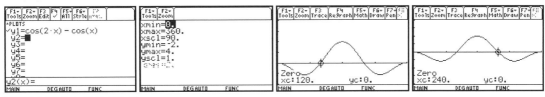

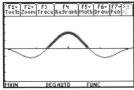

Answer: [120°, 240°] or {0°, 360°}

4.10 Maxima and Minima

1. $f(x) = 2x^2 + 1$ is defined in the interval $-3 \leq x \leq 3$. find minimum value of $f(x)$.

   Solution:

   Answer: 1

2. $f(x) = |3x + 1| - 1$ Find minimum value of $f(x)$.

   Solution:

   Answer: -1

3. $f(x) = -|x| + 3$ and $-2 \leq x \leq 4$ Find minimum value of $f(x)$ and the x value where this minimum

   occurs.

   Solution:

   Answer: $(4, -1)$

4. $y = \sqrt[3]{9 - x^2}$

   Find maximum value of y.

   Solution:

   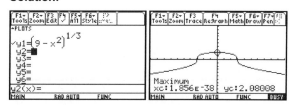

   Answer: 2.08

1. Find the domain of $f(x) = \log\sqrt{2x^2 - 15}$.

    Solution:

    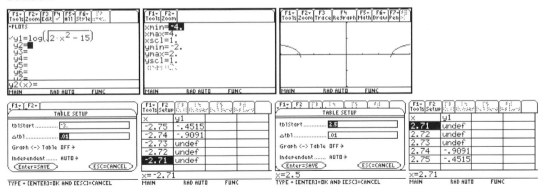

    Answer: Because of the even symmetry that the graph has and using the table, we deduce that the domain of the function is as follows: $x < -2.73$ or $x > 2.73$. This can also be stated as $|x| > 2.73$. Please note that the answer is accurate to the nearest hundredth.

2. Find domain and range of the function $y = x^{-4/3}$

    Solution:

    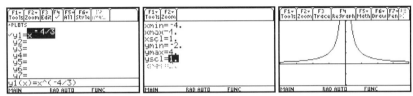

    Answer: Domain: $x \neq 0$; Range: $y > 0$.

3. Find the domain and range of the function $f(x) = 4 - \sqrt{2x^3 - 16}$

    Solution:

    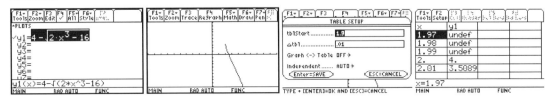

    Answer: Domain: $x \geq 2$; Range: $y \leq 4$.

4. If $f(x) = 2x^2 + 5x + 2$; $g(x) = 4x^2 - 4$ then what must be excluded from the domain of $\left(\dfrac{f}{g}\right)(x)$ for it be a function?

    Solution: The function $g(x)$ is the denominator of the given polynomial which must be nonzero.

    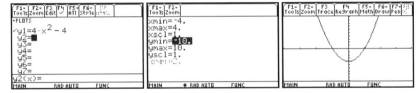

    Answer: The values that must be excluded from the domain are: -1 and 1.

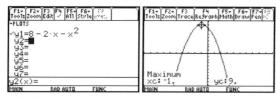

5.   Find range of $y = 8 - 2x - x^2$

Solution:

Answer: $y \leq 9$

6. $f(x) = \log(\sin x)$. Find domain of $f(x)$.

Solution:

In order that $f(x)$ be a function $\sin(x)$ must be positive.

$X\min = -4\pi$; $X\max = 4\pi$; $X\mathrm{scl} = \pi$

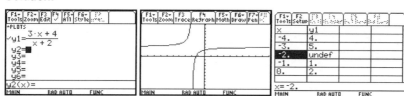

Answer: $2k\pi < x < (2k + 1)\pi$ where k is any integer.

7.   Find domain and range of $f(x) = \dfrac{3x + 4}{x + 2}$

Solution:

The function is undefined for $x = -2$.

The limit at positive and negative infinity is 3; therefore function has the horizontal asymptote $y = 3$.

Answer: Domain: $x \neq -2$; Range: $y \neq 3$.

8.   What value(s) must be excluded from the domain of $f(x) = \dfrac{x + 1}{2x - 2}$ and what is the range of $f(x)$?

Solution:

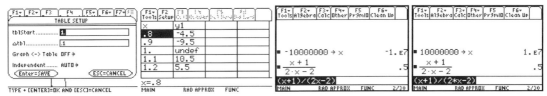

The function is undefined for x = 1; the limit at positive and negative infinity is 3; therefore function has the horizontal asymptote y = 0.5.

Answer: Domain: x ≠ 1; Range: y ≠ 0.5.

9. Find domain and range of y = $\sqrt{x^2 - 9}$.

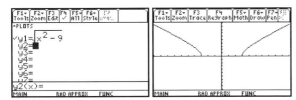

Answer: Domain: x ≤ −3 or x ≥ 3; range: y ≥ 0.

10. Find domain and range of y = $\sqrt{9 - x^2}$.

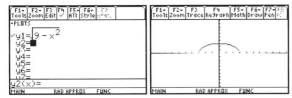

Answer: Domain: −3 ≤ x ≤ 3; Range: 0 ≤ y ≤ 3.

11. Domain of f(x) is given by $x^2 + 3x - 4 < 0$ and f(x) = $x^2 + 4x + 5$.

Find range of f(x).

Solution:

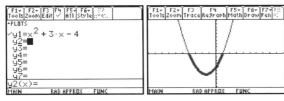

Domain: −4 < x < 1

Answer: 1 ≤ y < 10

4.12 Evenness and Oddness

State whether each of the following functions are even, odd, or neither. Make sure you display each function in a window where $x_{min} = -x_{max}$ and $y_{min} = -y_{max}$.

1. $f(x) = 2x^4$

    Solution:

    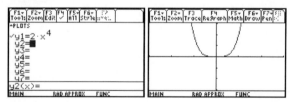

    Answer: Even (symmetric in the y – axis)

2. $f(x) = -x^2 + sinx$

    Solution: Angle mode: Radians

    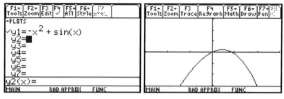

    Answer: Neither dd nor even (there is no symmetry in the origin; there is no symmetry in the y axis.

3. $f(x) = log(x^2)$

    Solution:

    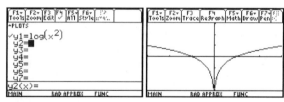

    Answer: Even

4. $f(x) = |x|$

    Solution:

    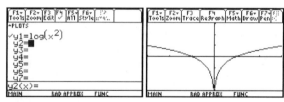

    Answer: Even

---

5. $f(x) = \dfrac{1}{x}$

Solution:

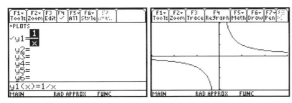

Answer: Odd (symmetric in the origin)

6. $f(x) = -x^5 - 8x^3 + 12x$

Solution:

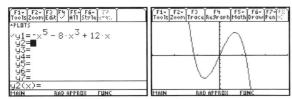

Answer: Odd

7. $f(x) = \cos x$ and $g(x) = 2x + 1$

Angle mode: Radians

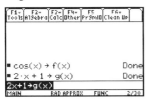

i) $f(x) \cdot g(x)$

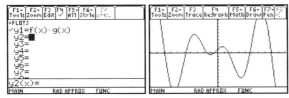

Answer: Neither odd nor even

ii) $f(g(x))$

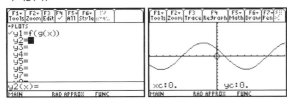

Answer: Neither odd nor even

iii) g(f(x))

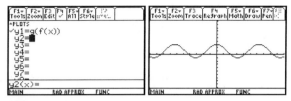

Answer: Even

8. $f(x) = \dfrac{1}{\sec x}$

Solution: Angle mode: Radians

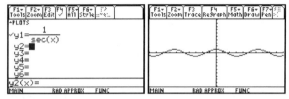

Answer: Even

9. $f(x) = \cos x$

Solution: Angle mode: Radians

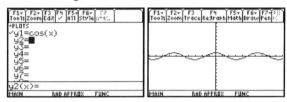

Answer: Even

10. $f(x) = \dfrac{1}{\csc(x)}$

Solution: Angle mode: Radians

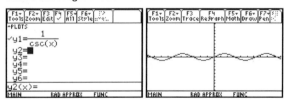

Answer: Odd

11. $f(x) = \sin x$

Solution: Angle mode: Radians

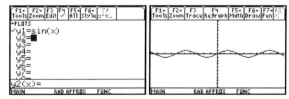

Answer: Odd

12. $f(x) = \sin x + 1$

Solution: Angle mode: Radians

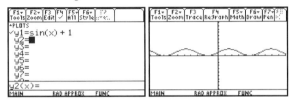

Answer: Neither odd nor even

13. $f(x) = x^4 - 3x^2 + 5$

Solution:

Answer: Even

14. $f(x) = 3x^3 + 5$

Solution:

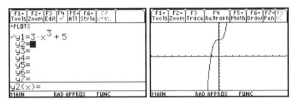

Answer: Neither odd nor even

15. $f(x) = 12x^6 + 4x^4 - 13x^2$

Solution:

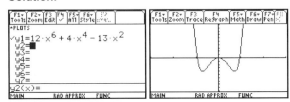

Answer: Even

16. $f(x) = x^3$

Solution:

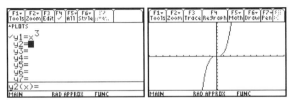

Answer: Odd

17. $f(x) = 3x^4 + 2x^2 - 8$

Solution:

Answer: Even

18. $y = 2$

Solution:

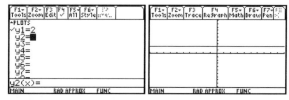

Answer: Even

19. $y = x$

Solution:

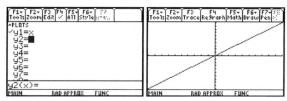

Answer: Odd

20. $f(x) = x^3 - 1$

Solution:

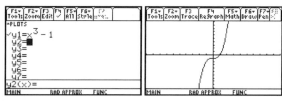

Answer: Neither odd nor even

21. $f(x) = x^2 - 1$

Solution:

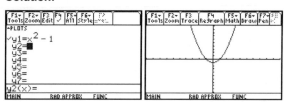

Answer: Even

22.　　$f(x) = -x + \sin x$

Solution: Angle mode: Radians

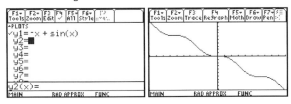

Answer: Odd

23.　　$f(x) = -x$

Solution:

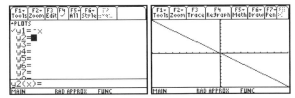

Answer: Odd

24.　　$f(x) = x^2 - \cos x$

Solution: Angle mode: Radians

Answer: Even

25.　　$f(x) = \dfrac{1}{x^2}$

Solution:

Answer: Even

26.　　$f(x) = x^3 + 1$

Solution:

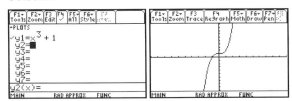

Answer: Neither odd nor even

27. $f(x) = \dfrac{x}{x - 2}$

Solution:

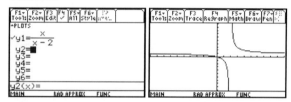

Answer: Neither odd nor even

28. $f(x) = x^3 + x$

Solution:

Answer: Odd

29. $f(x) = \sin(x)$

Solution: Angle mode: Radians

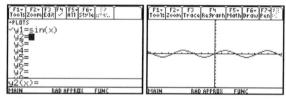

Answer: Odd

30. $f(x) = \sqrt{x^2 + 1}$

Solution:

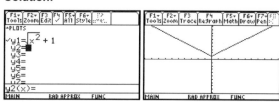

Answer: Even

Graphs of Trigonometric Functions

Most of the time one or more of the following are required concerning the graphs of the trigonometric functions. In order to find them all it is usually enough to find two adjacent maxima and the minimum point in between.

Period = The x – distance between two identical points in a periodic function; for example two adjacent maxima, minima or zeros.

Frequency = 1/Period

Amplitude = (Ymax – Ymin)/2

Offset = (Ymax + Ymin)/2

Axis of wave equation: y = Offset

1.   As x increases from 0 to π, what happens to $2\sin\dfrac{x}{2}$?

   Solution: Angle mode: Radians

   Answer: The function increases throughout in the given interval.

2.   What is the amplitude, Axis of wave and offset of y = 5sin(x) + 12cos(x) – 2?

   Solution: Angle mode: Radians

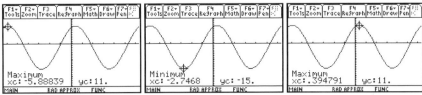

   Answer: Amplitude = (11 + 15)/2 = 13; Offset: (11 –15)/2 = –2; Axis of wave: y = –2

3.   What is the maximum value of $y = \sqrt{4 + \cos^2 x}$ in the interval $\left[\dfrac{-\pi}{2}, \dfrac{\pi}{2}\right]$?

   Solution: Angle mode: Radians

   Answer: 2.24

4.   Find y intercept of the function $y = \left| \sqrt{3}\sec\left[3(x + \frac{\pi}{4})\right] \right|$

Solution: Angle mode: Radians

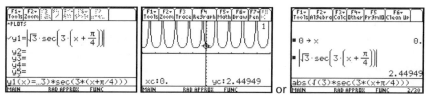

Answer: 2.45

5.   Find amplitude of the function $f(x) = -\frac{1}{2}\sin(x)\cos(x) + 1$

Solution: Angle mode: Radians

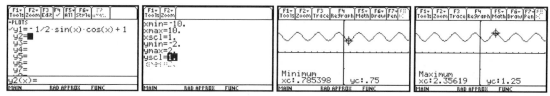

Answer: (1.25 – 0.75)/2 = 0.25

6.   Find the primary period of $f(x) = \dfrac{\cos(2x)}{1 + \sin(2x)}$

Solution: Angle mode: Radians

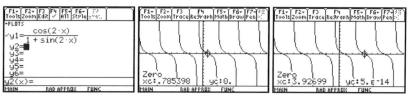

Answer: 3.93 – 0.79 = 3.14 → π

7.   Find primary period of $f(x) = 3\sin^2(2x)$

Solution: Angle mode: Radians

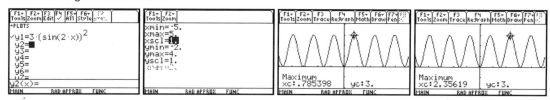

Answer: 2.36 – 0.79 = 1.57 → $\pi/2$

8.   Find y intercept of $y = \sqrt{3}\sin(x + \frac{\pi}{3})$

Solution: Angle mode: Radians

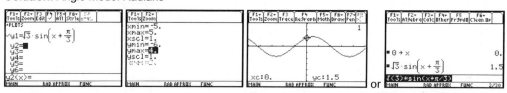

Answer: 1.5

---

9. What is the amplitude of the function y = 3sinx + 4cosx + 1

    Solution:

    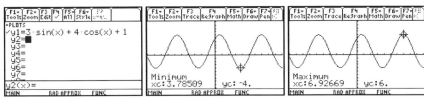

    Answer: (6 − (− 4))/2 = 5

10. Find maximum value of the function $f(x) = \sin(\frac{x}{4})$ over the interval $0 \le x \le \frac{\pi}{3}$

    Solution:

    Answer: 0.26

11. Find maximum value of 6 sinx cosx + 2

    Solution:

    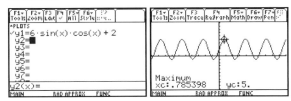

    Answer: 2

12. What happens to sinx as x increases from $-\frac{\pi}{4}$ to $\frac{3\pi}{4}$?

    Solution:

    Answer: The function increases between π/4 and π/2 and then decreases between π/2 and 3π/4.

13. What is the smallest positive x intercept of $y = 2\sin\left[3(x + \frac{3\pi}{4})\right]$?

    Solution:

    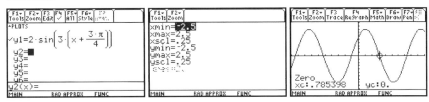

    Answer: 0.79 → π/4

---

14. What is the smallest positive angle that will make $y = 3 + \sin\left[3(x + \frac{\pi}{3})\right]$ a minimum?

Solution:

Answer: 0.52 → π/6

15. Find amplitude of the graph of the function $y = \cos^4 x - \sin^4 x + 1$

Solution:

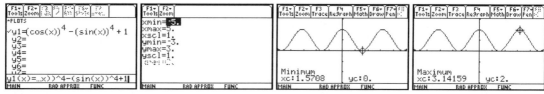

Answer: (2 − 0)/2 = 1

16. Find amplitude, period and frequency of the following:

a. $y = 2\sin(\pi x + \pi)$

Solution:

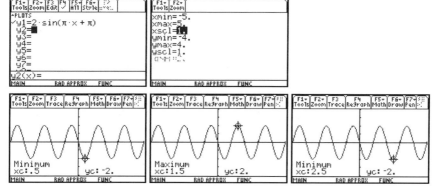

Answer: Amplitude = (2 − (−2))/2 = 2; Period = |2.5 − 0.5| = 2; Frequency = 1/2

b. $y = \frac{3}{4}\cos(\frac{x}{2} - \frac{\pi}{2})$

Solution:

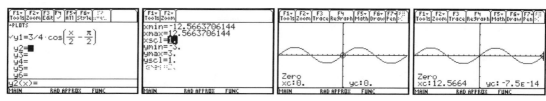

Period = 12.56 − 0 = 12.56 → 4π

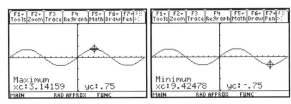

Answer: Frequency = 1/(4π); Amplitude = (0.75 − (−0.75))/2 = 0.75.

17. Find the coordinates of the first maximum point in the graph of $y = \sin(\frac{x}{2})$ that has a positive x −

coordinate.

Solution:

Answer: 3.14 → π

4.14 Miscellaneous Graphs

1. Find the point of intersection of the graphs $y = \log x$ and $y = \ln\dfrac{x}{2}$

   Solution:

   Answer: (3.41, 0.53)

2. At how many points does the function $y = x^3 + 5x - 2$ intersect the x axis?

   Solution:

   Answer: 1 point.

3. Plot the graph of $f(x) = \dfrac{x^2 - 1}{x - 1}$; locate the hole that the function has.

   Solution:

   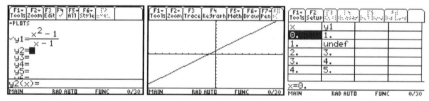

   Please note that at x = 1 the function is not defined and this is not a vertical asymptote, therefore the graph has a hole at that point.

4. Find x and y intercept(s) of the graph of equation $y = (x^2 - 4) \cdot \ln(x^2 + 9)$

   Solution:

   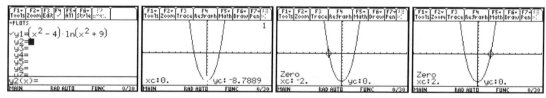

   Answer: y – intercept: (0, –8.79), x – intercepts: (–2, 0) and (2, 0)

5.   Determine which of the following functions has an inverse that is also a function.

a. $y = x^2 - 3x + 5$

Solution:

Answer: The inverse is not a function since the graph does not pass the horizontal line test, i.e. a horizontal line that cuts a certain graph at more than one point indicating that to one y value, more than one x values correspond. Such graphs do not correspond to one to one and onto functions. As a result the inverse is not a function.

b. $y = |x + 2| - 1$

Solution:

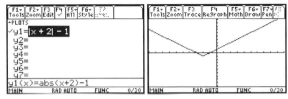

Answer: The inverse is not a function.

c. $y = \sqrt{16 - 9x^2}$

Solution:

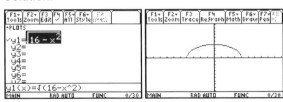

Answer: The inverse is not a function.

d. $y = x^3 + 5x - 2$

Solution:

Answer: The inverse is a function.

6. $f(x) = 2x^2 + 12x + 3$. If the graph of $f(x - k)$ is symmetric about the y axis, what is k?

Solution:

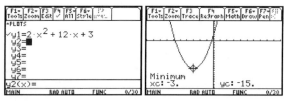

Answer: The graph must be shifted 3 units toward right therefore k = 3.

7.   Find equation of the axis of symmetry of $y = 3x^2 - x + 2$.

Solution:

Answer: The graph has the axis of symmetric of x = 0.17.

8.   What is the positive difference between the x and y intercept of the function given by $y = 2x^3 + x + 1$?

Solution:

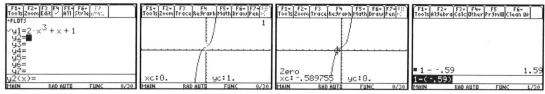

Answer: Positive difference is 1.59.

9. $y = -2x^2 + 4x - 7$. Determine the coordinates of the vertex of the parabola given above. Does the above function have a maximum or minimum? What is this value? Find the equation of the axis of symmetry also.

Solution:

Answer: The vertex is at (1, –5). This is also the maximum point of the graph. The graph doesn't have a minimum point since it is a downward parabola that tends to negative infinity. Equation of the axis of symmetry is x = 1 and it is a vertical line.

10. $f(x) = -(x - 1)^2 + 3$ and $-2 \le x \le 2$. Find the range of f(x).

Solution:

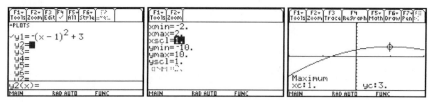

Answer: $-6 \le y \le 3$.

11. Plot the graphs and identify what each one represents:

a. $\dfrac{x^2}{9} + \dfrac{y^2}{4} = 1$ b. $\dfrac{x^2}{4} + \dfrac{y^2}{9} = 1$ c. $\dfrac{x^2}{9} - \dfrac{y^2}{4} = 1$ d. $\dfrac{y^2}{9} - \dfrac{x^2}{4} = 1$ e. $x^2 + (y-1)^2 = 4$

Solution:

Each of the following graphs is produced with the ZoomSqr option.

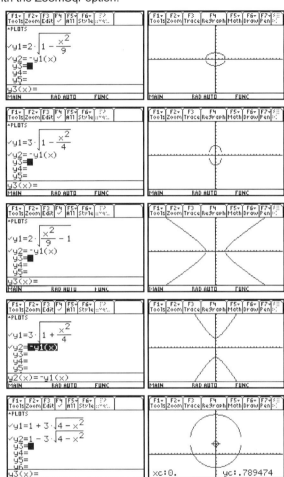

a. $\dfrac{x^2}{9} + \dfrac{y^2}{4} = 1 \Rightarrow y = \pm 2\sqrt{1 - \dfrac{x^2}{9}}$

This is an x – ellipse.

b. $\dfrac{x^2}{4} + \dfrac{y^2}{9} = 1 \Rightarrow y = \pm 3\sqrt{1 - \dfrac{x^2}{4}}$

This is a y – ellipse.

c. $\dfrac{x^2}{9} - \dfrac{y^2}{4} = 1 \Rightarrow y = \pm 2\sqrt{\dfrac{x^2}{9} - 1}$

This is an x – hyperbola.

d. $\dfrac{y^2}{9} - \dfrac{x^2}{4} = 1 \Rightarrow y = \pm 3\sqrt{1 + \dfrac{x^2}{4}}$

This is a y – hyperbola.

e. $x^2 + (y-1)^2 = 4 \Rightarrow y = 1 \pm \sqrt{4 - x^2}$

This is a circle.

1.   f(x) = k where k is an integer for which k ≤ x < k + 1 and g(x) = |f(x)| − f(x) + 1. What is the minimum value and the range for g(x)?

Solution:

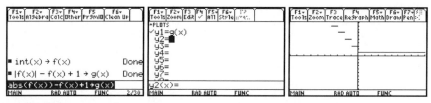

Answer: Minimum value 1, range: the set of positive odd integers

2.   g(x) = [x] − 2x + 1 what is the period of g(x)?

Solution:

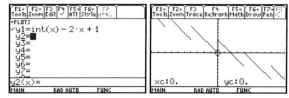

Answer: The function is not periodic.

3.   [4.6] − [−5.4] + 2[0.3] + [4] − [0] = ?

Solution:

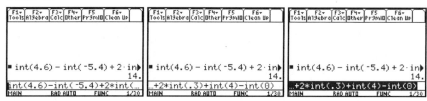

Answer: 14

4.   f(x) = |1 − 2x + 2[x]|

What is the period and frequency of the above function if [x] represents the greatest integer less than or equal to x? What are the maximum and the minimum values of f(x)? What is the amplitude, offset, and equation of the Axis of wave? What is the domain and range?

Solution:

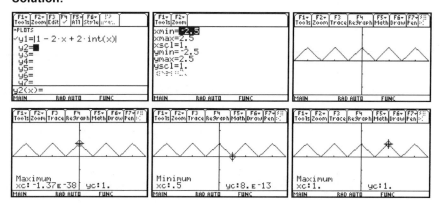

Answer: Min = 0; Max = 1

Period = |1 − 0| = 1 → (The distance between two adjacent maxima or minima)

Frequency = 1 → (Frequency = 1/Period)

Amplitude = (1 − 0)/2 = ½ → (Amplitude = (Ymax − Ymin)/2)

Offset: (1 + 0)/2 = ½ → (Offset = (Ymax + Ymin)/2)

Axis of wave: y = ½ → (Axis of wave equation is y = Offset)

Domain: R, Range: 0 ≤ y ≤ 1.

5.   f(x) = [x] where [x] represents the greatest integer function. What is the range of f(x)?

Solution:

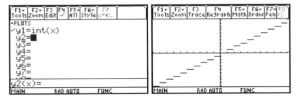

Answer: The range is all integers. The domain is all real numbers.

4.16 Parametric Graphs

Plot each of the following graphs and state what it represents.

1. $x = 4\cos\theta + 1; y = 3\sin\theta - 1$

   Solution:

   Function Mode: Parametric; Angle Angle mode: Radians; Tmin = -2π

   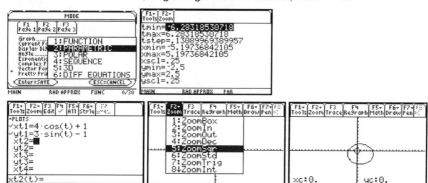

   Answer: The curve represents an ellipse.

2. $x = t^2 + t + 1; y = t^2 - t + 1$

   Solution:

   Function Mode: Parametric; Tmin = -2π; Zoom = ZoomSqr

   Answer: The curve represents a parabola.

3. $x = t^3 + 2; y = \dfrac{4}{3}t^3 + 1$

   Solution:

   Function Mode: Parametric; Tmin = -2π; Zoom = ZoomSqr

   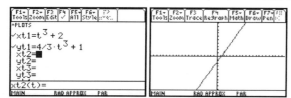

   Answer: The curve represents a line.

4. $x = t^2; y = 2t^2 - 1$

Solution:

Function Mode: Parametric; Tmin = -2π; Zoom = ZoomSqr

Answer: The curve represents (the positive x) portion of a line that starts at (0, –1).

5. $x = \sin\theta; y = \cos\theta$

Solution:

Function Mode: Parametric; Tmin = -2π; Zoom = ZoomSqr

Answer: The curve represents the unit circle.

6. $x = t; y = \sqrt{4 - t^2}$

Solution:

Function Mode: Parametric; Tmin = -2π; Zoom = ZoomSqr

Answer: The curve represents a semicircle.

7. $x = \sqrt{p}$ and $y = \sqrt{4 - p}$

Solution:

Function Mode: Parametric; Tmin = -2π; Zoom = ZoomSqr

Answer: The curve represents a quarter circle.

8.   x = 2sinα; y = 2sinα

Solution:

Function Mode: Parametric; Tmin = –2π; Zoom = ZoomSqr

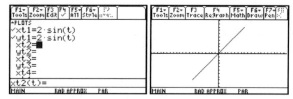

Answer: The curve represents portion of a line (ranging from (–2, –2) to (2, 2) since 2sinα takes the values between –2 and 2 inclusive).

9.   x = 2sinα; y = 2cosα

Solution:

Function Mode: Parametric; Tmin = –2π; Zoom = ZoomSqr

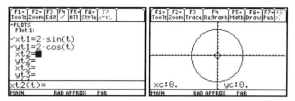

Answer: The curve represents a circle.

10.   x = 3sinα; y = 4cosα

Solution:

Function Mode: Parametric; Tmin = –2π; Zoom = ZoomSqr

Answer: The curve represents an ellipse (a y – ellipse).

11.   x = 3t + 4; y = t – 6

Solution:

Function Mode: Parametric; Tmin = –2π; Zoom = ZoomSqr

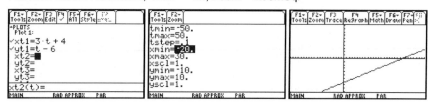

Answer: The curve represents a line.

12. $x = \sin^2 t$; $y = 3\cos t$

Solution:

Function Mode: Parametric; Tmin = -2π; Zoom = ZoomSqr

Answer: The curve represents portion of a parabola.

13. $x = t(1 + t)$; $y = t(-1 + t)$

Solution:

Function Mode: Parametric; Tmin = -2π; Zoom = ZoomSqr

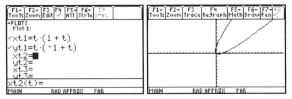

Answer: The curve represents a parabola.

14.   Using parametric equations plot the set of points (x^2, y) where $y = x^2 + 1$

Solution:

Function Mode: Parametric; Tmin = -2π; Zoom = ZoomSqr

(x^2, y) where $y = x^2 + 1$ is equivalent to $(x^2, x^2 + 1)$, thus:

$x = T^2$; $y = T^2 + 1$

Answer: The curve represents a portion of a line.

15.   Using parametric equations plot the set of points (x^2, y) where $y = 2x - 1$.

Solution:

Function Mode: Parametric; Tmin = -2π; Zoom = ZoomSqr

$x = T^2$; $y = 2T - 1$

Answer: The curve represents a parabola.

16. Plot the inverse of the following function using parametric equations. y = 2x³ + x + 1

Solution:

Function Mode: Parametric; Tmin = –2π; Zoom = ZoomSqr

Answer:

Please note that in order to plot the inverse of the given function we switch x and y.

1. What is the area enclosed by the following curves and the coordinate axes?

$$r = \frac{3}{\sin\theta}$$

$$r = \frac{4}{\cos\theta}$$

Solution:

Function Mode: Polar

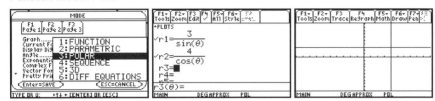

Answer: 4·3 = 12

2. $r = \dfrac{4}{\dfrac{1}{\sec\theta} + 2\sin\theta}$ what is the area of the region bounded by the above curve and the x and y axes?

Solution:

Function Mode: Polar

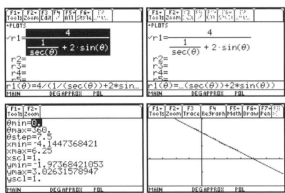

Answer: 2·4/2 = 4

3. What is the area of the region that the curve r = 3cosθ represents?

Solution:

Function Mode: Polar

Answer: $\pi \cdot 1.5^2 = 2.25\pi = 7.07$

1. $$\lim_{x \to \infty} \frac{3x^4 - 5x^3 + 8}{-4x^4 + 7x^2 + 4x + 5} = ?$$

Solution:

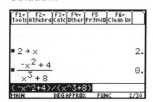

Answer: -0.75

2. $$\lim_{x \to \infty} \frac{6x^3 + 5x^2 - 8x}{-2x^2 + 1} = ?$$

Solution:

Answer: $-\infty$

3. $$\lim_{x \to -\infty} \frac{x^3 - 27}{x^4 - 81} = ?$$

Solution:

Answer: 0

4. $$\lim_{x \to 2} \frac{-x^2 + 4}{x^3 + 8} = ?$$

Solution:

Answer: 0

5. $\lim\limits_{x \to 3} \dfrac{x^3 - 27}{x^4 - 81} = ?$

Solution:

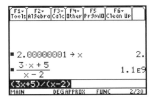

Answer: 0.25

6. $\lim\limits_{x \to 2^+} \dfrac{3x + 5}{x - 2} = ?$

Solution:

Answer: $+\infty$

7. $\lim\limits_{x \to 2} \dfrac{3x + 5}{x - 2} = ?$

Solution:

Answer: Limit does not exist because the right hand limit and the left hand limits are not the same.

8. $\lim\limits_{x \to 0} \dfrac{\sin(3x)}{\tan(2x)} = ?$

Solution:

Answer: 1.5

9. $\lim\limits_{x \to 1} \dfrac{x-1}{\ln x} = ?$

Solution:

| F1▾ F2▾ F3▾ F4▾ F5 F6▾ |
| Tools A19ebra Calc Other Pr9mIO Clean Up |
| ■ 1.0000001 → x   1. |
| ■ $\dfrac{x-1}{\ln(x)}$ 1. |
| ■ .99999999 → x   1. |
| ■ $\dfrac{x-1}{\ln(x)}$ 1. |
| (x-1)/(ln(x)) |
| MAIN   DEG APPROX   FUNC   4/30 |

Answer: 1

10. $\lim\limits_{x \to 0^+} x^x = ?$

Solution:

| F1▾ F2▾ F3▾ F4▾ F5 F6▾ |
| Tools A19ebra Calc Other Pr9mIO Clean Up |
| |
| |
| ■ 1.E⁻8 → x   1.E⁻8 |
| ■ x^x 1. |
| x^x |
| MAIN   DEG APPROX   FUNC   2/30 |

Answer: 1

11. $f(x) = \begin{cases} \dfrac{4x^2 + 3x}{x} & x \neq 0 \\ m & x = 0 \end{cases}$

If f(x) is a continuous function then m = ?

Solution:

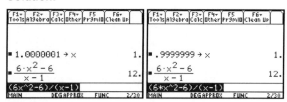

F1▾ F2▾ F3▾ F4▾ F5 F6▾		F1▾ F2▾ F3▾ F4▾ F5 F6▾
Tools A19ebra Calc Other Pr9mIO Clean Up		Tools A19ebra Calc Other Pr9mIO Clean Up
■ 1.E⁻6 → x .000001		■ -1.E⁻5 → x -.00001
■ $\dfrac{4 \cdot x^2 + 3 \cdot x}{x}$ 3.		■ $\dfrac{4 \cdot x^2 + 3 \cdot x}{x}$ 2.99996
(4*x^2+3*x)/x		(4*x^2+3*x)/x
MAIN DEG APPROX FUNC 2/30		MAIN DEG APPROX FUNC 2/30

Answer: 3

12. $f(x) = \begin{cases} \dfrac{6x^2 - 6}{x-1} & x \neq 1 \\ A & x = 1 \end{cases}$

If f(x) is a continuous function then A = ?

Solution:

F1▾ F2▾ F3▾ F4▾ F5 F6▾		F1▾ F2▾ F3▾ F4▾ F5 F6▾
Tools A19ebra Calc Other Pr9mIO Clean Up		Tools A19ebra Calc Other Pr9mIO Clean Up
■ 1.0000001 → x 1.		■ .9999999 → x 1.
■ $\dfrac{6 \cdot x^2 - 6}{x-1}$ 12.		■ $\dfrac{6 \cdot x^2 - 6}{x-1}$ 12.
(6x^2-6)/(x-1)		(6*x^2-6)/(x-1)
MAIN DEG APPROX FUNC 2/30		MAIN DEG APPROX FUNC 2/30

Answer: 12

13. In order to be continuous at x = 2 what must $f(x) = \dfrac{x^4 - 16}{x^3 - 8}$ be defined to be equal to?

Solution:

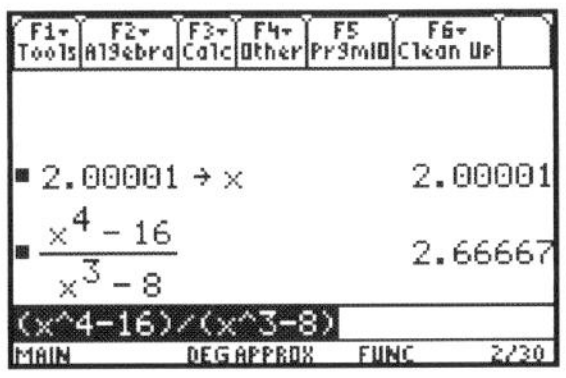

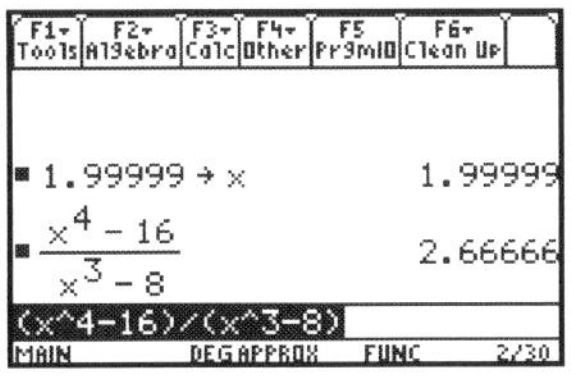

Answer: 8/3

4.19 Horizontal and Vertical Asymptotes

1. Find the horizontal and vertical asymptotes as well as the domain and range of:

(a) $y = \dfrac{2x^2 - 18}{x^2 - 4}$

Solution:

The function has a local minimum at the point (0, 4.5).

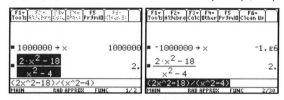

The limits at positive and negative infinity are both equal to 2. Therefore the function has a horizontal asymptote at x = 2.

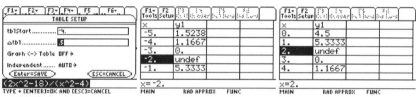

The function has two vertical asymptotes: x = −2 and x = 2.

Answer:

Horizontal asymptote: y = 2   **Domain:** All real numbers except −2 and 2

Vertical asymptotes: x = −2 and x = 2   **Range:** y < 2 or y ≥ 4.5.

(b) $y = \dfrac{3x^2 - 3x - 6}{x^2 - 4}$

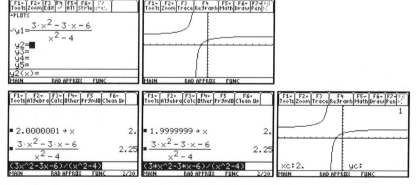

The function has a hole at x = 2; it is the point (2, 2.25).

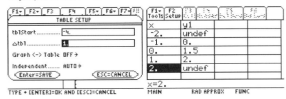

The limits at positive and negative infinity are both equal to 3. Therefore the function has a horizontal asymptote at x = 3.

The function has one vertical asymptote at x = –2 (and a hole at x = 2).

Answer:

Horizontal asymptote: y = 2.25   **Domain:** All real numbers except –2 and 2

Vertical asymptote: x = –2   **Range:** y ≠ 3 and y ≠ 2.25.

(c) $y = \dfrac{x+2}{x^2 - 4}$

Solution:

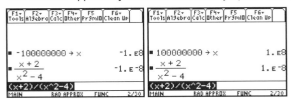

The function apparently has one vertical asymptote and one horizontal asymptote.

The limits at positive and negative infinity are both equal to 0. Therefore the function has a horizontal asymptote at x = 0.

The function has one vertical asymptote at x = 2 and a hole at (–2, –0.25).

Answer:

Horizontal asymptote: $y = 0$ **Domain:** All real numbers except -2 and 2

Vertical asymptote: $x = 2$ **Range:** $y \neq 0$ and $y \neq -0.25$.

(d) $y = \dfrac{x^2 - 4x - 5}{x^2 - 1}$

Solution:

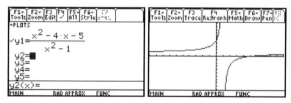

The function apparently has one vertical asymptote and one horizontal asymptote.

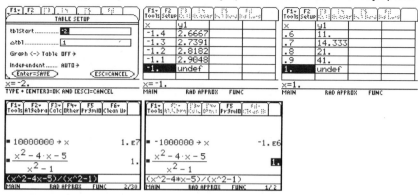

The limits at positive and negative infinity are both equal to 1. Therefore the function has a horizontal asymptote at $x = 1$.

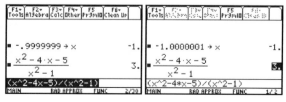

The function has a hole at $(-1, 3)$.

Answer:

Horizontal asymptote: $y = 1$ **Domain:** All real numbers except -1 and 1

Vertical asymptote: $x = 1$ **Range:** $y \neq 1$ and $y \neq 3$.

(e) $y = \dfrac{x + 3}{(x - 3)(x^2 - 9)}$

Solution:

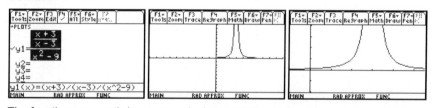

The function apparently has one vertical asymptote and one horizontal asymptote.

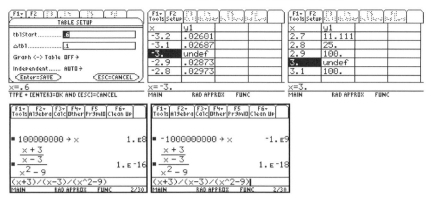

The limits at positive and negative infinity are both equal to 0. Therefore the function has a horizontal asymptote at x = 0.

Answer:

Horizontal asymptote: y = 0

Vertical asymptote: x = 3

Domain: All real numbers except –3 and 3

Range: y > 0 (Although the graph is undefined at x = –3, because of its symmetry about the line x = 3, the y value of 0.0278 exists in the range with the corresponding x value of 9. Therefore the value 0.0278 is not excluded from the range.

2. Find equations of the vertical asymptotes of f(x) = $\dfrac{x^2 + 4x + 3}{x + 2} \cdot \dfrac{1}{\cot(\pi x)}$

Solution:

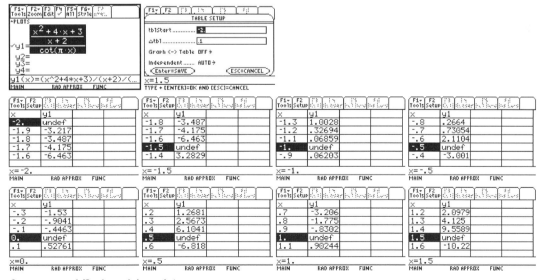

Answer: x = k/2 where k is an integer.

1. $4(\text{cis}70^\circ)^4 = ?$

   Solution: Angle mode: Degrees

   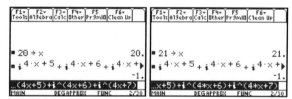

   Answer: $0.69 - 3.94i$

2. $f(x) = 3x^5 - 2x^3 + 8x - 2;\ f(i) = ?$

   Solution:

   ```
   F1▾  F2▾  F3▾  F4▾  F5   F6▾
   Tools Algebra Calc Other Pr9mIO Clean Up

   ■ 3·x^5 - 2·x^3 + 8·x - 2 → f(x)
                                 Done
   ■ f(i)                  -2. + 13.·i
   f(i)
   MAIN      DEG APPROX    FUNC    2/30
   ```

   Answer: $-2 + 13i$

3.   If n is an arbitrary positive integer then $i^{4n+5} + i^{4n+6} + i^{4n+7} = ?$

   Solution:

   ```
   F1▾  F2▾  F3▾  F4▾  F5   F6▾          F1▾  F2▾  F3▾  F4▾  F5   F6▾
   Tools Algebra Calc Other Pr9mIO Clean Up   Tools Algebra Calc Other Pr9mIO Clean Up

   ■ 20 → x              20.          ■ 21 → x              21.
   ■ i^(4·x+5) + i^(4·x+6) + i^(4·x▸)  ■ i^(4·x+5) + i^(4·x+6) + i^(4·x▸)
                        -1.                                -1.
   ...(4x+5)+i^(4x+6)+i^(4x+7)        ...x+5)+i^(4*x+6)+i^(4*x+7)
   MAIN    DEG APPROX  FUNC  2/30     MAIN    DEG APPROX  FUNC  2/30
   ```

   Answer: -1

4. $i^{192} + i^{193} + i^{194} + i^{195} = ?$

   Solution:

   ```
   F1▾  F2▾  F3▾  F4▾  F5   F6▾
   Tools Algebra Calc Other Pr9mIO Clean Up

   ■ i^192 + i^193 + i^194 + i^195
                                 0.
   i^192+i^193+i^194+i^195
   MAIN      DEG APPROX    FUNC    1/30
   ```

   Answer: 0

5.   What is the reciprocal of $3 + 4i$

   Solution:

   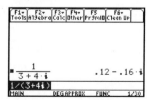

   Answer: $0.12 - 0.16i$

6. $\dfrac{1+i}{6i+8} = ?$

Solution:

Answer: 0.14 + 0.02i

7. $z = 3\text{cis}\dfrac{\pi}{8}$; $z^3 = ?$

Solution: Angle mode: Radians

Answer: 10.33 + 24.94i

8. $z = \dfrac{1+i\sqrt{3}}{-1+i\sqrt{3}}$, what is the value of z in trigonometric form?

Solution: Angle mode: Degrees

Answer: 1*(cos(−60°) + isin(−60°))

9.   A = 3cis40°; B = 4(cos50° + isin50°); A·B = ?

Solution:

Answer: 12i

1. $_5P_2 + {}^6P_3 + P(5, 3) = ?$

    Solution:

    Answer: 200

2. $\binom{5}{3} + C_2^8 + {}_6C_3 = ?$

    Solution:

    Answer: 58

3. $\dfrac{(6+3)!}{6! + 3!}$

    Solution:

F1▾	F2▾	F3▾	F4▾	F5	F6▾
Tools	Algebra	Calc	Other	PrgmIO	Clean Up

    ■ $\dfrac{(6+3)!}{6!+3!}$ 499.835

    (6+3)!/(6!+3!)

    MAIN   DEG APPROX   FUNC   1/30

    Answer: 499.83

1. $\cos(2\sin^{-1}(\frac{-5}{13})) = ?$

    Solution:

    Answer: 0.70

2. $f(x) = \sin(\cos(x)); f(320^\circ) = ?$

    Solution:

    Angle mode: Radians

    OR

    Calculate cos(320) in degree mode, then calculate sin(0.766044) in radian mode:

    Answer: 0.693

3. $f(x) = 14x^2; g(x) = f(\cos x) + f(\tan x); g(12^\circ) = ?$

    Solution: Mode Degrees

    Answer: 14.03

4. $\cos 30\cdot\cos 30^\circ - \sin 45\cdot\sin 45^\circ = ?$

    Solution: Mode Radians

    Answer: −0.47

---

5. $f(r, \theta) = r\cos\theta$; $f(12, 13) = ?$

   Solution: Angle mode: Radians

   Answer: 10.89

6. $\csc(\tan^{-1}\dfrac{1}{\sqrt{2}}) = ?$

   Solution:

   Answer: 1.73

7. $\text{Arcsin}0.6 + \cos^{-1}0.6 = ?$

   Solution: Mode Radians

   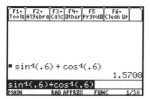

   Answer: 1.57

8. $\cos x = \dfrac{1}{3} \Rightarrow \sqrt{\sec x} = ?$

   Solution:

   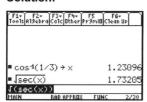

   Answer: 1.73

9. $\left.\begin{array}{l} f(x,y) = \tan(x) + \tan(y) \\ g(x,y) = 1 - \tan(x)\cdot\tan(y) \end{array}\right\} \dfrac{f(10°,20°)}{g(10°,20°)} = ?$

   Solution: Mode Degrees

   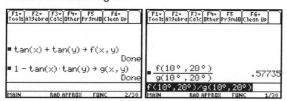

   Answer: 0.577

10. $\cos A = 0.6631$ and $\tan A = -1.12884 \Rightarrow A = ?$ (in degrees)

Solution: Mode Degrees

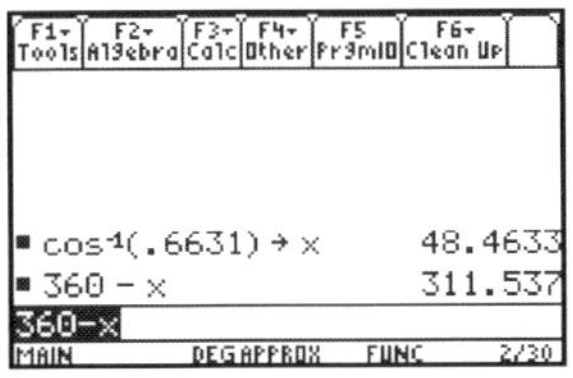
cos⁻¹(.6631) → x 48.4633
360 − x 311.537
360-x
MAIN DEG APPROX FUNC 2/30

Answer: 311.54°

11. sec 4.1 = x; csc(3 Arctanx) = ?

Solution: Angle mode: Radians

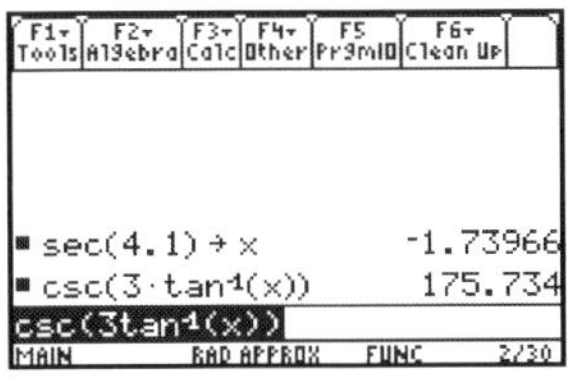
sec(4.1) → x -1.73966
csc(3·tan⁻¹(x)) 175.734
csc(3tan⁻¹(x))
MAIN RAD APPROX FUNC 2/30

Answer: 175.73

12. $\sin A = \dfrac{5}{13}$ and $90^\circ \le A \le 180^\circ$; $\cos B = \dfrac{4}{9}$, B is in 4'th quadrant; $\sin(A + B) = ?$

Solution: Angle mode: Degrees

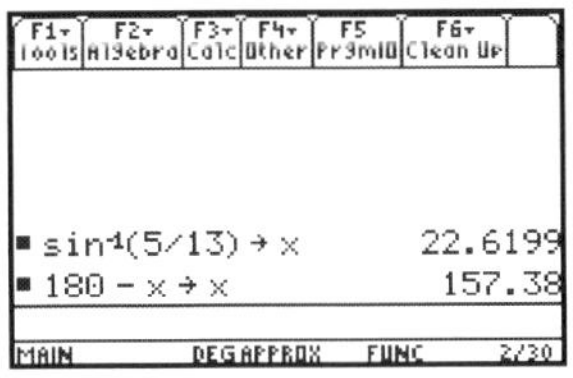
sin⁻¹(5/13) → x 22.6199
180 − x → x 157.38
MAIN DEG APPROX FUNC 2/30
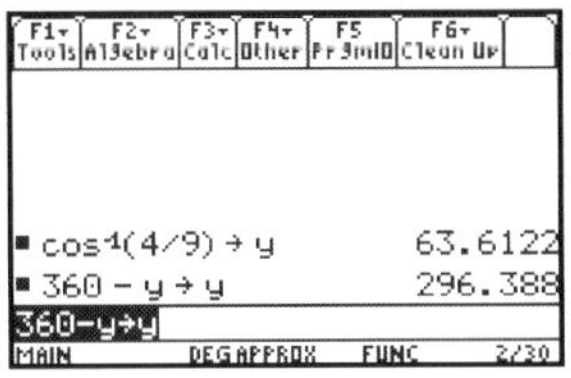
cos⁻¹(4/9) → y 63.6122
360 − y → y 296.388
360-y→y
MAIN DEG APPROX FUNC 2/30
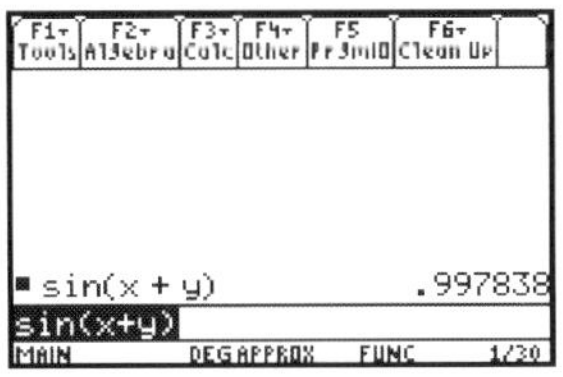
sin(x + y) .997838
sin(x+y)
MAIN DEG APPROX FUNC 1/30

Answer: 0.9978

13. In which quadrant is the angle represented by Arcsin($\dfrac{-3}{5}$) + Arccos($\dfrac{-12}{13}$)?

Solution: Mode Degrees

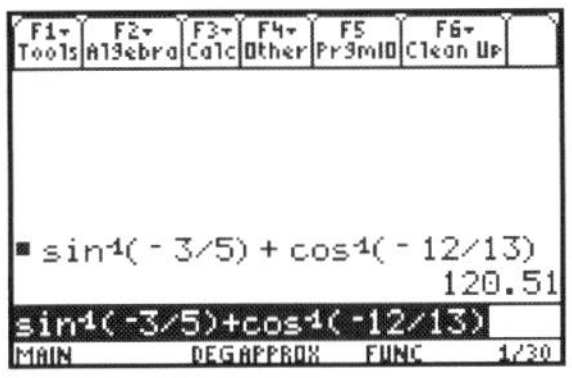
sin⁻¹(-3/5) + cos⁻¹(-12/13)
120.51
sin⁻¹(-3/5)+cos⁻¹(-12/13)
MAIN DEG APPROX FUNC 1/30

Answer: 2nd quadrant

14. $A \# B = \sqrt{\cos A + \sec B}$; 4 # 5 = ?

Solution: Angle mode: Radians

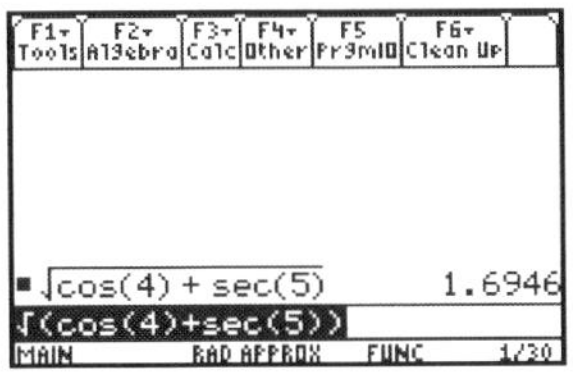
√(cos(4) + sec(5)) 1.6946
√(cos(4)+sec(5))
MAIN RAD APPROX FUNC 1/30

Answer: 1.69

15. $\dfrac{\cos 15^\circ}{\sin 75^\circ} = ?$

Solution: Angle mode: Degrees

Answer: 1

16. $\dfrac{\tan 25^\circ}{\cos 65^\circ} = ?$

Solution: Angle mode: Degrees

Answer: 1.10

17. $\cos 210^\circ = ?$

Solution: Angle mode: Degrees

■ cos(210)   -.866025
cos(210)
MAIN   DEG APPROX   FUNC   1/30

Answer: – 0.87

18. $\cos(\tan^{-1}(1/3)) = ?$

Solution:

■ cos(tan⁻¹(1/3))   .948683
cos(tan⁻¹(1/3))
MAIN   RAD APPROX   FUNC   1/30

Answer: 0.95

19. $$\frac{\sin 135° \cdot \cos \frac{5\pi}{6}}{\tan 225°} = ?$$

Solution: Angle mode: Radians

Answer: − 0.61

20. $\csc\theta = \dfrac{4}{3}$; $\cos\theta < 0$; $\tan\theta = ?$

Solution: Angle mode: Degrees

Answer: −1.134

21. $\cos 310° + \sin 140° = 2x \Rightarrow x = ?$

Solution: Angle mode: Degrees

![Two calculator screens showing solve(cos(310) + sin(140) = 2·x, x) with x = .642788]

Answer: 0.64

22. $\sin 330° = ?$

Solution: Angle mode: Degrees

![Calculator screen showing sin(330) = -.5]

Answer: − 0.5

23. $\cos \pi - \sin 930° - \csc \left(\dfrac{-5\pi}{2}\right) + \sec(0°) = ?$

Solution: Angle mode: Radians

Answer: 1.5

24. $\tan(-135°) + \cot\left(\dfrac{-7\pi}{8}\right) = ?$

Solution: Angle mode: Radians

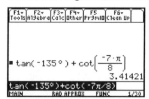

Answer: 3.41

25. $\sec\dfrac{7\pi}{6} \cdot \tan\dfrac{3\pi}{4} \cdot \sin\dfrac{2\pi}{3} = ?$

Solution: Mode Radians

Answer: 1

26.   Given that $\tan\theta = \dfrac{-5}{12}$ and $\sin\theta$ is positive. $\cos(2\theta) - \sin(180° - \theta) = ?$

Solution: Angle mode: Degrees

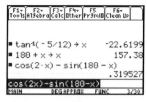

Answer: 0.320

27. A is in 3rd quadrant and tan A = $\dfrac{8}{15}$; B is in 2nd quadrant and tan B = $\dfrac{-3}{4}$. In which quadrant does (A + B) lie?

Solution: Angle mode: Degrees

F1▾ Tools	F2▾ Algebra	F3▾ Calc	F4▾ Other	F5 PrgmIO	F6▾ Clean Up	
▪ tan⁻¹(8/15) → x						28.0725
▪ 180 + x → x						208.072
▪ tan⁻¹(-3/4) → y						-36.8699
▪ 180 + y → y						143.13
▪ x + y						351.203

x+y
MAIN   DEG APPROX   FUNC   5/30

Answer: 4th quadrant

28. tan θ = $\dfrac{3}{4} \Rightarrow \sin θ = ?$

Solution: Angle mode: Degrees

F1▾ Tools	F2▾ Algebra	F3▾ Calc	F4▾ Other	F5 PrgmIO	F6▾ Clean Up	
▪ tan⁻¹(3/4) → x						36.8699
▪ sin(x)						.6
▪ sin(180 + x)						-.6

sin(180+x)
MAIN   DEG APPROX   FUNC   3/30

Answer: ±0.6

29. sin A = $\dfrac{3}{5}$ and cos A < 0; tan(2A) = ?

Solution: Angle mode: Degrees

F1▾ Tools	F2▾ Algebra	F3▾ Calc	F4▾ Other	F5 PrgmIO	F6▾ Clean Up	
▪ sin⁻¹(3/5) → x						36.8699
▪ 180 - x → x						143.13
▪ tan(2·x)						-3.42857

tan(2x)
MAIN   DEG APPROX   FUNC   3/30

Answer: −3.43

30. $\cos^2 20° - \sin^2 20° = ?$

Solution: Angle mode: Degrees

F1▾ Tools	F2▾ Algebra	F3▾ Calc	F4▾ Other	F5 PrgmIO	F6▾ Clean Up	
▪ (cos(20))² - (sin(20))²						
						.766044

(cos(20))^2-(sin(20))^2
MAIN   DEG APPROX   FUNC   1/30

Answer: 0.77

31. A and B are acute angles and tan(A) = $\dfrac{12}{5}$ and sin(B) = $\dfrac{4}{5} \Rightarrow \cos(2A + B) = ?$

Solution:

F1▾ Tools	F2▾ Algebra	F3▾ Calc	F4▾ Other	F5 PrgmIO	F6▾ Clean Up	
▪ tan⁻¹(12/5) → a						67.3801
▪ sin⁻¹(4/5) → b						53.1301
▪ cos(2·a + b)						-.990533

cos(2a+b)
MAIN   DEG APPROX   FUNC   3/30

Answer: −0.99

32.   i. $\cos\theta = \dfrac{4}{5}$; $\sin(2\theta) = ?$ $\tan(2\theta) = ?$

Solution: Angle mode: Degrees

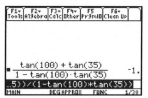

Answer: $\sin(2\theta) = \pm0.96$ and $\tan(2\theta) = \pm3.43$

ii. $\theta = \cos^{-1}\dfrac{4}{5}$; $\sin(2\theta) = ?$ $\tan(2\theta) = ?$

Solution: Angle mode: Degrees

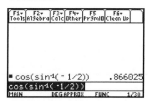

Answer: $\sin(2\theta) = 0.96$ and $\tan(2\theta) = 3.43$

33. $\dfrac{\tan100^{o} + \tan35^{o}}{1 - \tan100^{o} \cdot \tan35^{o}} = ?$

Solution: Angle mode: Degrees

Answer: -1

34. $\cos(\sin^{-1}(\dfrac{-1}{2})) = ?$

Solution:

Answer: 0.87

35. **Important Note:** The answers for the following questions are given in both Degree and Radian values as both of them may be asked in the test. It should be noted, however, that these are not two separate answers, but different representations of the same correct answer.

a. $\sin^{-1}\dfrac{1}{2} = ?$

Solution:

Answer: 0.52 Radians or 30° Degrees

b. $\sin^{-1}\dfrac{-\sqrt{3}}{2} = ?$

Solution:

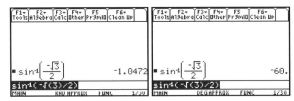

Answer: –1.05 Radians or –60° Degrees

c. $\cos^{-1}\dfrac{\sqrt{3}}{2} = ?$

Solution:

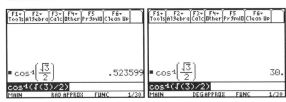

Answer: 0.52 Radians or 30° Degrees

d. $\text{Arccos}\dfrac{-\sqrt{3}}{2} = ?$

Solution:

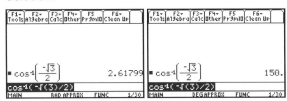

Answer: 2.62 Radians or 150° Degrees

e. $\tan^{-1}(1) = ?$

Solution:

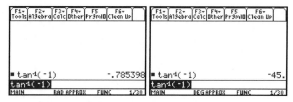

Answer: 0.79 Radians or 45° Degrees

f. $\text{Arctan}(-1) = ?$

Solution:

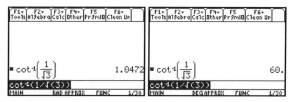

Answer: −0.79 Radians or −45° Degrees

g. $\cot^{-1}(\dfrac{1}{\sqrt{3}}) = ?$

Solution:

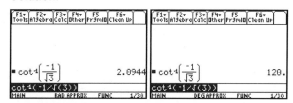

Answer: 1.05 Radians or 60° Degrees

h. $\cot^{-1}(\dfrac{-1}{\sqrt{3}}) = ?$

Solution:

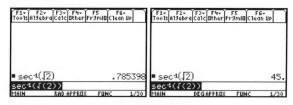

Answer: 2.09 Radians or 120° Degrees

i. $\sec^{-1}(\sqrt{2}) = ?$

Solution:

Answer: 0.79 Radians or 45° Degrees

j. $\sec^{-1}(-\sqrt{2}) = ?$

Solution:

Answer: 2.36 Radians or 135° Degrees

k. $\csc^{-1}(2) = ?$

Solution:

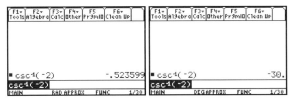

Answer: 0.52 Radians or 30° Degrees

l. $\csc^{-1}(-2) = ?$

Solution:

Answer: −0.52 Radians or −30° Degrees

36. $\sin(\text{Arccos}\ \dfrac{4}{5}) = ?$

Solution:

Answer: 0.6

37. $\cos(\text{Arcsin}\ \dfrac{-4}{5} + \text{Arccos}\ \dfrac{12}{13}) = ?$

Solution:

Answer: 0.86

38. $f(x) = \sin x;\ f^{-1}(\frac{3\pi}{14}) = ?$

Solution: Mode Radians

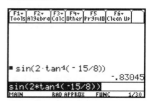

Answer: 0.74

39. $\sin(2\arctan(\frac{-15}{8})) = ?$

Solution:

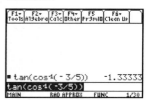

Answer: −0.83

40. $\tan(\text{Arccos}\ \frac{-3}{5}) = ?$

Solution:

Answer: −1.33

41. a. $\text{Arccos}(\cos \frac{7\pi}{6}) = ?$

Solution: Angle mode: Radians

Answer: 2.62

b. Arctan(tan $\frac{\pi}{4}$) = ?

Solution: Angle mode: Radians

Answer: 0.79

c. Arctan(tan $\frac{5\pi}{4}$) = ?

Solution: Angle mode: Radians

Answer: 0.79

42. f(x) = e^x; g(x) = cos x; (fog)($\sqrt{3}$) = ?

Solution: Angle mode: Radians

Answer: 0.85

43. f(x) = $\sqrt{2x-2}$; g(x) = cosx; g^{-1}(f($\sqrt{2}$)) = ?

Solution: Angle mode: Radians

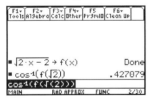

Answer: 0.427

44. $\sqrt{2002 \cdot 2003 - 2001 \cdot 2002}$ = ?

Solution:

Answer: 63.28

45. $f(x, y) = 2x^2 - y^2$; $g(x) = 5^x$; $g(f(4, 3)) = ?$

Solution:

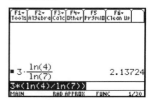

Answer: $1.2 \cdot 10^{16}$

46. $f(x, y) = \sqrt{3x^2 - 4y}$; $g(x) = 3^x$; $g(f(2, 1)) = ?$

Solution:

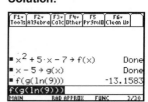

Answer: 22.36

47. $f(x) = \sqrt{3x - 4}$ and $g(x) = x^3 + x + 1$; $f(g(2)) = ?$

Solution:

Answer: 5.39

48. $f(x) = 3x$; $f(\log_7 4) = ?$

Solution:

Answer: 2.14

49. $f(x) = x^2 + 5x - 7$; $g(x) = x - 5$; $f(g(\ln 9)) = ?$

Solution:

Answer: −13.16

50. $f(x) = \sqrt{x}$; $g(x) = \sqrt[3]{(x+2)^2}$; $h(x) = \sqrt[5]{x-4}$; $h(g(f(2))) = ?$

Solution:

Answer: -1.12

51. $f(x) = x \ln x$; $g(x) = 10^{x+1}$; $g(f(3)) = ?$

Solution:

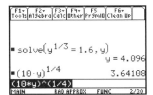

Answer: 19762.27

52. $a\Omega b = \dfrac{a}{e + \dfrac{\pi}{b}}$; $(2\ \Omega\ 3)\ \Omega\ 4 = ?$

Solution:

![TI-89 screen: e^1 → e 2.71828; 2/(e+π/3) → x .531141][TI-89 screen: 2/(e+π/3) → x .531141; x/(e+π/4) .151595; x/(e+π/4)]

Answer: 0.15

53. $\sin^{-1}(\cos 200°) = ?$

Solution: Angle mode: Degrees

![TI-89 screen: sin⁻¹(cos(200)) -70.; sin⁻¹(cos(200))]

Answer: -70

54. $\sqrt[3]{y} = 2.6$; $\sqrt[4]{10y} = ?$

Solution:

![TI-89 screen: solve(y^(1/3)=1.6,y) y=4.096; (10·y)^(1/4) 3.64108; (10*y)^(1/4)]

Answer: 3.64

---

55. $\left(\dfrac{28}{34}\right)^{\frac{-5}{6}} = ?$

Solution:

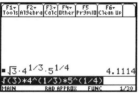

Answer: 1.18

56. $\sqrt{3} \cdot \sqrt[3]{4} \cdot \sqrt[4]{5} = ?$

Solution:

Answer: 4.11

57. $a \lozenge b = \dfrac{\sqrt[3]{a} + \sqrt[3]{2b} - 1}{\sqrt{ab - 1}} ; \ 3 \lozenge \pi = ?$

Solution:

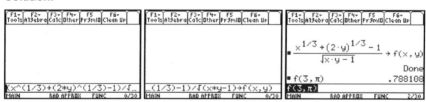

Answer: 0.79

58. $f(x) = x\sqrt[3]{x} \ ; \ (f(\sqrt{2}) = ?$

Solution:

Answer: 1.59

59. $x_o = \sqrt{2} \ ; \ x_{n+1} = x_n \sqrt[3]{x_n + 2} \ ; \ x_3 = ?$

Solution:

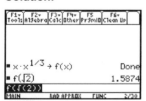

Answer: 6

60. $f(x) = \sqrt[3]{x}$; $g(x) = x^4 + 2$; $(fog)(4) = ?$

Solution:

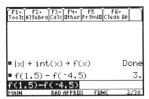

Answer: 6.366

61. $3^{4/3} + 4^{5/4} = ?$

Solution:

Answer: 9.98

65. $f(x) = |x| + [x]$; $f(1.5) - f(-4.5) = ?$

Solution:

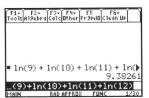

Answer: 3

66. $\log_4(\cos 290°) = ?$

Solution:

Answer: $- 0.77$

67. $\sum\limits_{i=9}^{12} \ln i = ?$

Solution:

Answer: 9.38

68. $\log(\sin2) + \log(\sin20) + \log(\sin20°) = ?$

Solution: Angle mode: Radians

| F1▾ Tools | F2▾ A1gebra | F3▾ Calc | F4▾ Other | F5 PrgmIO | F6▾ Clean Up | | | F1▾ Tools | F2▾ A1gebra | F3▾ Calc | F4▾ Other | F5 PrgmIO | F6▾ Clean Up | | | F1▾ Tools | F2▾ A1gebra | F3▾ Calc | F4▾ Other | F5 PrgmIO | F6▾ Clean Up |

$$\blacksquare \log(\sin(2)) + \log(\sin(20)) \rightarrow$$
$$-.546798$$

```
log(sin(2))+log(sin(20))+...     ...g(sin(20))+log(sin(20°))     ...g(sin(20))+log(sin(20°))
MAIN    RAD APPROX    FUNC  0/30  MAIN   RAD APPROX   FUNC   0/30  MAIN   RAD APPROX   FUNC   1/30
```

Answer: -0.55

69. $F(x, y) = \log_y x$; $F(e, \pi^2) = ?$

Solution:

| F1▾ Tools | F2▾ A1gebra | F3▾ Calc | F4▾ Other | F5 PrgmIO | F6▾ Clean Up |

$$\blacksquare \frac{\ln(x)}{\ln(y)} \rightarrow f(x, y) \qquad \text{Done}$$
$$\blacksquare e^1 \rightarrow e \qquad 2.71828$$
$$\blacksquare f(e, \pi^2) \qquad .436784$$

```
f(e,π^2)
MAIN    RAD APPROX    FUNC   3/30
```

Answer: 0.44

70. $\log_{36}6 - \log_3 27 + \log_2(0.25)^{1/3} = ?$

Solution:

| F1▾ Tools | F2▾ A1gebra | F3▾ Calc | F4▾ Other | F5 PrgmIO | F6▾ Clean Up | | | F1▾ Tools | F2▾ A1gebra | F3▾ Calc | F4▾ Other | F5 PrgmIO | F6▾ Clean Up | | | F1▾ Tools | F2▾ A1gebra | F3▾ Calc | F4▾ Other | F5 PrgmIO | F6▾ Clean Up |

$$\blacksquare \frac{\ln(6)}{\ln(36)} - \frac{\ln(27)}{\ln(3)} + \frac{\ln(.25)}{\ln(2)}$$
$$-3.16667$$

```
ln(6)/ln(36)-ln(27)/ln(3)...    ...n(3)+ln(.25^(1/3))/ln(2)    ...n(3)+ln(.25^(1/3))/ln(2)
MAIN    RAD APPROX   FUNC  0/30  MAIN   RAD APPROX   FUNC   0/30  MAIN   RAD APPROX   FUNC   1/30
```

Answer: -3.17

71. $\log_{\sqrt{5}} 4 - \log_{16}\sqrt{125} = ?$

Solution:

| F1▾ Tools | F2▾ A1gebra | F3▾ Calc | F4▾ Other | F5 PrgmIO | F6▾ Clean Up |

$$\blacksquare \frac{\ln(4)}{\ln(\sqrt{5})} - \frac{\ln(\sqrt{125})}{\ln(16)} \qquad .851983$$

```
...(√(5))-ln(√(125))/ln(16)
MAIN    RAD APPROX   FUNC   1/30
```

Answer: 0.85

72. $f(x) = x^4 - 88 x^3 - 1134 x^2 + 3888x + 56135$; $f(99) = ?$

Solution:

| F1▾ Tools | F2▾ A1gebra | F3▾ Calc | F4▾ Other | F5 PrgmIO | F6▾ Clean Up |

$$\blacksquare 99 \rightarrow x \qquad 99.$$
$$\blacksquare x^4 - 88 \cdot x^3 - 1134 \cdot x^2 + 3888$$
$$2.$$

```
...8x^3-1134x^2+3888x+56135
MAIN    RAD APPROX   FUNC   2/30
```

Answer: 2

73. $f(x) = x^3 - 4x^2 + 6x - 4$; $f(3) - f(\sqrt{3}) = ?$

Solution:

Answer: 5.41

Men do less than they ought, unless they do all they can.
Thomas CARLYLE

First say to yourself what you would be;and then do what you have to do.

EPICTETUS

Page 136

CHAPTER 5.

MODEL TESTS

We are all inventors, each sailing out on a voyage of discovery, guided each by a private chart, of which there is no duplicate. The world is all gates, all opportunities.

Ralph Waldo EMERSON

SAT Math Level 1 – Model Test

Test Duration: 60 Minutes

Directions: For each of the following problems, decide which is the best of the choices given. If the exact numerical value is not one of the choices, select the choice that best approximates this value. Then fill in the corresponding oval on the answer sheet.

Notes:

- A calculator will be necessary for answering some (but not all) of the questions in this test. For each question you will have to decide whether or not you should use a calculator. The calculator you use must be at least a scientific calculator; programmable calculators and calculators that can display graphs are permitted.

- The only angle measure used on this test is degree measure. Make sure your calculator is in the degree mode.

- Figures that accompany problems in this test are intended to provide information useful in solving the problems. They are drawn as accurately as possible except when it is stated in a specific problem that its figure is not drawn to scale.

- All figures lie in a plane unless otherwise indicated.

- Unless otherwise specified, the domain of any function f is assumed to be the set of all real numbers x for which f(x) is a real number.

Reference Information: The following information is for your reference in answering some of the questions in this test.

- Volume of a right circular cone with radius r and height h: $V = \frac{1}{3}\pi r^2 h$

- Lateral area of a right circular cone with circumference of the base c and slant height l: $S = \frac{1}{2}cl$

- Volume of a sphere with radius r: $V = \frac{4}{3}\pi r^3$

- Surface area of sphere with radius r: $S = 4\pi r^2$

- Volume of a pyramid with base area B and height h: $V = \frac{1}{3}Bh$

1. If $k = \frac{1}{\sqrt{2}}$ and $p = \frac{1-k}{1+k}$ then what is the value of p?

(A) $3 + 2\sqrt{2}$ (B) $3 - 2\sqrt{2}$ (C) $2 - 3\sqrt{2}$ (D) $2 + 3\sqrt{2}$ (E) $3 + 3\sqrt{2}$

2 If $f(x) = x^3 - 5x + k$ and $f(-2) = 5$ then which of the following is the value of k?

(A) –8   (B) 2   (C) 3   (D) 5   (E) 10

3. If $|x - 3| = 5$ then which of the following can be $|x + 3| + 1$?

(A) 1   (B) 2   (C) 8   (D) 10   (E) 11

4. Which of the following is correct for the function given by f(x) = x² – 4?

   I. f(x) = f(–x)   II. f(–x) = – f(x)   III. f(–2) < f(0)

(A) I only   (B) II only   (C) III only   (D) I and III only   (E) I, II and III

5. If a and b are two distinct nonzero real numbers for which $a \cdot b = \frac{a}{b} = a - b$ then what is the value of a + b?

(A) –3/2   (B) –3/4   (C) 0   (D) 1/2   (E) 2/3

6. If $\frac{\sin^2 x + \cos^2 x}{\sin(2x)} = 2.18$ and x is an acute angle then which of the following can be the degree measure of x?

(A) 13.7   (B) 23.7   (C)27.3   (D) 63.7   (E) 67.3

7. If f(sin(x)) = cos²x then which of the following can be f(x)?

(A) 1 – x   (B) 1 – x²   (C) x² – 1   (D) $\frac{1}{1-x^2}$ (E) $\frac{1}{x^2-1}$

8. If a function f(x) and its inverse f⁻¹(x) are equal, then f(x) is symmetric across

(A) the x axis   (B) the y axis   (C) the origin   (D) the line y = x   (E) the line y = –x

9. If two distinct numbers are selected from the set {23, 34, 45, 56, 67} then what is the probability that their sum will be less than 100?

(A) 0.3   (B) 0.4   (C) 0.5   (D) 0.6   (E) 0.9

10. A mathematician gives the following answer when one of his friends asks his age: "My age today equals the sum of the digits of the year when I was born." If this conversation was made in the year 2005 then which of the following can be the year when the mathematician was born?

(A) 1972   (B) 1976   (C) 1979   (D) 1981   (E) 1984

11. If the graph of f(x) passes through the origin, then which of the following points must be on the graph of f(x – 2) + 2?

(A) (–2, 2)   (B) (2, –2)   (C) (2, 2)   (D) (–2, –2)
(D) None of the above

12. If f(x) = x⁴ – 4x³ – 8x² + 6, then for how many real numbers r does f(r) = 1?

(A) 0   (B) 1   (C) 2   (D) 3   (E) 4

13. If 3 – 4i is one of the roots of a polynomial P(x) with real coefficients, then which of the following must also be a root of P(x) given that i = $\sqrt{-1}$?

(A) –3 – 4i   (B) –3 + 4i   (C) 4 + 3i   (D) 3 + 4i
(E) It cannot be determined from the information given.

14. In order to find the solutions of the equation f(x) = g(x), which of the following can be performed?

   I.   Graphing both functions on the same set of axes and finding the x–coordinate of each of the points where the functions intersect.

   II. Graphing both functions on the same set of axes and finding the y–coordinate of each of the points where the functions intersect.

   III. Graphing the function f(x) – g(x) and finding the x intercepts.

(A) I only   (B) II only   (C) I and II only   (D) I and III only   (E) I, II and III

15. Sets A, B and C given in figure 1 contain the integer multiples of 4, 6 and 10 respectively. If the shaded region that represents the intersection of the three sets contains the integer multiples of the positive integer n, then what is the smallest value of n?

Figure 1

(A) 30   (B) 60   (C) 90   (D) 120   (E) 240

16. What is the equation of the circle centered at (1, –3) and tangent to the y axis?

(A) $(x - 1)^2 + (y + 3)^2 = 9$ (B) $(x + 1)^2 + (y - 3)^2 = 9$ (C) $(x + 1)^2 + (y - 3)^2 = 1$

(D) $(x - 1)^2 + (y + 3)^2 = 1$ (E) $(x - 3)^2 + (y + 1)^2 = 1$

17. What is the diameter of the sphere whose volume is 100 cm^3?

(A) 1.44 cm   (B) 2.88 cm   (C) 5.67   (D) 5.76 cm   (E) 11.52 cm

18. The functions f(x) and g(x) are given by $f(x) = \dfrac{3}{2x}$ and $g(x) = \dfrac{3}{2x + 2}$. Which of the following is the correct relation between the graphs of f(x) and g(x)?

(A) The graph of g(x) can be obtained by shifting the graph of f(x) by 2 units in the leftward direction.

(B) The graph of g(x) can be obtained by shifting the graph of f(x) by 2 units in the rightward direction.

(C) The graph of g(x) can be obtained by shifting the graph of f(x) by 1 unit in the leftward direction.

(D) The graph of g(x) can be obtained by shifting the graph of f(x) by 1 unit in the rightward direction.

(E) The graph of g(x) can be obtained by shifting the graph of f(x) by 1 unit in the upward direction.

19. The height of a stone dropped from a certain height is given as a function of time by h(t) = 100 – 5t^2 where h(t) is the height in meters t seconds after the stone was released. How many seconds later does the stone fall to 55 m?

(A) 1   (B) 2   (C) 3   (D) 4   (E) 5

20. If x is a negative real number for which $\log_3\left(x^2 - 5x - 5\right) = 2$ then x = ?

(A) –7   (B) –5   (C) –2   (D) 2   (E) 7

21. Which of the following cannot be the range of a function whose domain is {1, 2, 3, 4}?

(A) {0}   (B) {–10, 10}   (C) {–1, –2, –3}   (D) {1, 2, 3, 4, 5}   (E) {101, 102, 103, 104}

22. How many of the distinct factors of 504 are odd?

(A) 6   (B) 12   (C) 18   (D) 24   (E) 48

23. Which of the following graphs correctly gives the solution set of the inequality $\dfrac{(x-1)\cdot(x+2)^2}{x-3} \geq 0$?

(A)

(B)

(C)

(D)

(E)

24. Point C whose coordinates are (1, 8) is on the parabola defined by $f(x) = p - x^2$ as shown in figure 2. What is the area of the trapezoid given if AB || DC?

(A) 24   (B) 32   (C) 48   (D) 64

(E) It cannot be determined from the information given.

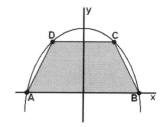

Figure 2

Figure not drawn to scale

25. In January 2000, the population in town Rushville was 24, 800. Assuming a growth rate of 5 percent per year, what will be the population growth from January 2006 to January 2007 rounded to the nearest ten people?

(A) 1650   (B) 1660   (C) 1670   (D) 1680   (E) 1690

26. A line m passes through the origin and point A where point A has the coordinates of(91, 79). How many points on line m have integral coordinates and lie between origin and point A?

(A) None   (B) 1   (C) 2   (D) 3   (E) More than 3

27. If f(x) = |2x − 4| then which of the following gives all real values of x for which f(x) is less than x?

(A) $\dfrac{4}{3} < x < 4$ (B) $x < 4$ (C) $x > \dfrac{4}{3}$ (D) $-4 < x < 4$ (E) $-\dfrac{4}{3} < x < \dfrac{4}{3}$

28. If $\sqrt{x}$ is approximated by $\dfrac{x}{14} + \dfrac{7}{2}$ then what is the percentage of the error made while evaluating $\sqrt{63}$?

(A) 0.6   (B) 0.7   (C) 0.8   (D) 0.9   (E) 1

29. A person, standing 18 ft away from the base of a tree, sights the top of the tree with an angle of elevation that equals 28.65 degrees. Which of the following is the height of the tree in feet assuming that the person's eyes are 6 ft above the ground level?

(A) 6.16   (B) 9.38   (C) 9.83   (D) 15.16   (E) 15.83

30. The average price of n books is x dollars. What will be the average price of the remaining books when two books are excluded if each of these two books is priced at y dollars?

(A) $\dfrac{n \cdot x - 2 \cdot y}{n}$
(B) $\dfrac{x - 2 \cdot y}{n - 2}$
(C) $\dfrac{n \cdot x - 2 \cdot y}{n - 2}$
(D) $\dfrac{n \cdot x}{n - 2}$
(E) $\dfrac{n - 2}{n \cdot x - 2 \cdot y}$

31. Which of the following functions satisfies the relation $f(x) = f(|x|)$?

    I. $f(x) = x^4 - x^2 + 1$ II. $f(x) = 4x^2 + 2x$ III. $f(x) = \ln(x^2)$

(A) I only
(B) II only
(C) III only
(D) I and II only
(E) I and III only

32. In figure 3, AB is both the diameter of the smaller semicircle and the radius of the greater quarter circle. Segment CE is parallel to segment BA and is tangent to the smaller semicircle at point F. What is the measure of the angle ABE indicated by α?

(A) 15   (B) 25   (C) 30   (D) 45   (E) 60

Figure 3

33. A salesman who works in Serra Fashion Wear is paid the weekly wages of $350 plus a 6.5% bonus of his sales in that week. In order to earn $600 in a particular week, what is the total amount of sales that this salesman should make?

(A) 3468   (B) 3648   (C) 3486   (D) 3846   (E) 3864

34. A line m passes through the origin and is perpendicular to line n given by $x + 3y = p$. If lines m and n intersect at the point $(r, r + 1)$ then $r = ?$

(A) –5   (B) –0.5   (C) 0.5   (D) 4   (E) 5

35. The circle given in figure 4 passes through vertices A, B, and C of the triangle and BC is the diameter of the circle. If the coordinates of A and C are (1, 3.5) and (4, –0.7) respectively then what is the slope of AB?

(A) 1.4   (B) –1.4   (C) 5/7   (D) –5/7

(E) It cannot be determined from the information given.

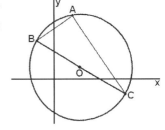

Figure 4

36. The function given in figure 5 is rotated about the x axis for 180°. What is the volume of the resulting solid?

(A) 2.09   (B) 3.14   (C) 4.19   (D) 6.28   (E) 8.38

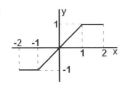

Figure 5

37. For the rectangular box given in figure 6, x is the smallest acute angle in the shaded triangle; tanx + cosx = ?

   (A) 0.56   (B) 0.87   (C) 1.43   (D) 1.79   (E) 2.67

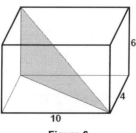

Figure 6

Figure not drawn to scale

38. The graph given in figure 7 represents the parabola $x = ay^2 + by + c$. Which of the following must be correct?

   (A) $a < 0$, $c > 0$ and $b^2 - 4ac < 0$ (B) $a < 0$, $c < 0$ and $b^2 - 4ac > 0$

   (C) $a < 0$, $c > 0$ and $b^2 - 4ac > 0$ (D) $a > 0$, $c > 0$ and $b^2 - 4ac < 0$

   (E) $a > 0$, $c > 0$ and $b^2 - 4ac > 0$

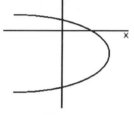

Figure 7

39. Given that A, B and C are three distinct digits where the 8 digit number 44ABC920 is the product of six consecutive multiples of three then which of the following can be A + B + C?

   (A) 8   (B) 12   (C) 17   (D) 20   (E) 26

40. How many distinct triangles are there in figure 8?

   (A) 6   (B) 8   (C) 10   (D) 12   (D) 14

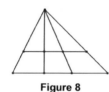

Figure 8

41. In an attempt to solve for x in the equation $\sqrt{x-2} = x - 8$ a student squares both sides of the equation. Which of the following assumptions does the student make?

(A) x is a real number less than 8   (B) x is a positive real number

(C) x is a real number greater than 8   (D) x is a nonnegative real number

(E) x is a real number greater than or equal to 8

42. When simplified $\cos\theta \cdot \left(\dfrac{1}{1-\sin\theta} - \dfrac{1}{1+\sin\theta}\right)$ equals which of the following?

   (A) $\tan\theta$ (B) $\sec\theta$ (C) $\csc\theta$ (D) $2\cdot\tan\theta$ (E) $2\cdot\sec\theta$

43. If in figure 9 lines l, m, and n are parallel then x = ?

   (A) 2.5   (B) 3   (C) 3.5   (D) 4.5   (E) 5

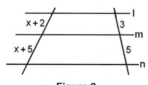

Figure 9

44. Which of the following is not logically equivalent to the statement given by "If f(a) = f(b), then a = b"?

(A) If a ≠ b, then f(a) ≠ f(b).   (B) f(a) = f(b) is a sufficient condition for a = b.

(C) If a = b, then f(a) = f(b).   (D) a = b is a necessary condition for f(a) = f(b).

(E) f(a) ≠ f(b) or a = b.

45. The graph of y = |f(x)| is given in figure 10. Which of the following can be f(x)?

(A) $-x^2 - 2x + 3$ (B) $x^2 + 2x + 3$ (C) $x^2 - 2x - 3$ (D) $x^2 - 1$ (E) $-x^2 - 2x$

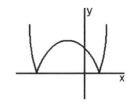

Figure 10

46. In figure 11, line m is the axis of symmetry of both the equilateral triangle ABC and the square DEFG. If the individual lengths of the minor arcs CF, FB and BE are x, y and z respectively, which of the following is correct?

(A) x : y : z = 3 : 5 : 1   (B) x : y : z = 7 : 11 : 2

(C) x : y : z = 3 : 5 : 2   (D) x : y : z = 6 : 10 : 3

(E) x : y : z = 4 : 6 : 2

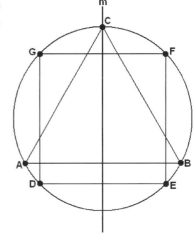

Figure 11

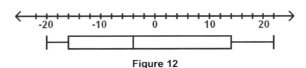

Figure 12

47. Pertaining to the data summarized by the box and whisker plot in figure 12, which of the following assertions may be false about the data?

(A) Median of the numbers in the data is negative.

(B) Data contains both positive and negative numbers.

(C) Range of the numbers in the data is greater than 40.

(D) More than half of the numbers in the data are negative.

(E) Half of the numbers in the data lie between −16 and 14 inclusive

48. A spider is at vertex A of the 3 in by 5 in by 6 in block of marble shown in figure 13 and it is heading towards vertex B. What is the length of the shortest path from A to B to the nearest tenth of an inch?

(A) 10   (B) 10.3   (C) 10.8   (D) 11.7   (E) 14

Figure 13

49. Based on the information given in figure 14, what is the length of the segment indicated by x?

(A) 5.94   (B) 6.04   (C) 6.24   (D) 6.42

(E) It cannot be determined from the information given.

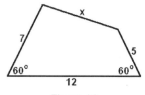

Figure 14

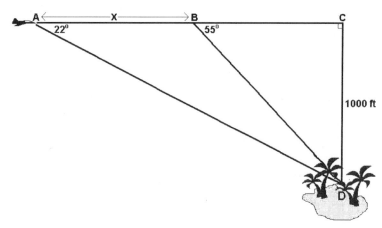

Figure 15

50. A plane cruising at an altitude of 1000 ft sights an island at the angle of depression of 22° at point A and 55° at point B as indicated in figure 15 above. What is the horizontal distance x between A and B rounded to the nearest 10 yards?

(A) 580   (B) 590   (C) 600   (D) 1770   (E) 1780

S T O P
END OF TEST

SAT Math Level 2 – Model Test

Test Duration: 60 Minutes

Directions: For each of the following problems, decide which is the best of the choices given. If the exact numerical value is not one of the choices, select the choice that best approximates this value. Then fill in the corresponding oval on the answer sheet.

Notes:

- A calculator will be necessary for answering some (but not all) of the questions in this test. For each question you will have to decide whether or not you should use a calculator. The calculator you use must be at least a scientific calculator; programmable calculators and calculators that can display graphs are permitted.

- For some questions in this test you may have to decide whether your calculator should be in the radian mode or the degree mode.

- Figures that accompany problems in this test are intended to provide information useful in solving the problems. They are drawn as accurately as possible except when it is stated in a specific problem that its figure is not drawn to scale.

- All figures lie in a plane unless otherwise indicated.

- Unless otherwise specified, the domain of any function f is assumed to be the set of all real numbers x for which f(x) is a real number.

Reference Information: The following information is for your reference in answering some of the questions in this test.

- Volume of a right circular cone with radius r and height h: $V = \dfrac{1}{3}\pi r^2 h$

- Lateral area of a right circular cone with circumference of the base c and slant height l: $S = \dfrac{1}{2}cl$

- Volume of a sphere with radius r: $V = \dfrac{4}{3}\pi r^3$

- Surface area of sphere with radius r: $S = 4\pi r^2$

- Volume of a pyramid with base area B and height h: $V = \dfrac{1}{3}Bh$

1. The sum and product of two positive real numbers x and y are both 10. What is the smaller number?

(A) 1.127   (B) 1.217   (C) 1.712   (D) 8.837   (E) 8.873

2. If $\log_{25}(x^2 + y^2) = 2$, and x = 7, then y = ?

(A) –24 only   (B) 24 only   (C) –24 or 24 only   (D) –7 only   (E) –7 or 7 only

3. The functions f(x) and –f(x) are symmetric across

(A) the line given by y = x   (B) the origin   (C) the x axis

(D) the line given by y = –x   (E) the y axis

4. If $\dfrac{x^2 - y + 1}{x - 2} = 0$ then y cannot equal

(A) –5   (B) –4   (C) –2   (D) 5

(E) It cannot be determined from the information given.

5. Which of the following vectors is perpendicular to the vector whose endpoints are given by (–1, 2) and (3, –1)?

(A) (4, 3)   (B) (–3, –4)   (C) (–4, 3)   (D) (8, –6)   (E) (–8, 6)

6. Which of the following can not intersect in more than 2 points?

(A) A sphere and a circle   (B) A parabola and a plane   (C) A circle and a cube

(D) A line and a parabola   (E) An ellipse and a circle

7. What does the graph of Ax + By = C represent when A and B are nonzero and C is zero?

(A) A line passing through origin   (B) The y axis

(C) A vertical line other than the y axis   (D) The x axis

(E) A horizontal line other than the x axis

8. If $\left(\sqrt{3} + x\right)\left(\sqrt{y} - 4\right) = 0$ then which of the following is the least possible value of $x^2 + y^2$?

(A) 2   (B) 3   (C) 4   (D) 16   (E) 19

9. A quadratic function f(x) has two real and distinct roots x_1 and x_2. If the sum and product of x_1 and x_2 are both negative, then which of the following can be the graph of f(x)?

(A)   (B)   (C)   (D)   (E)

 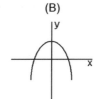

10. How many horizontal or vertical lines intersect the function $f(x) = \dfrac{x}{x^2 - x}$ at no points?

(A) 1   (B) 2   (C) 3   (D) 4   (E) More than 4

11. What is the primary period of the function f(x) = p·sin(qx) given that p and q are both positive real numbers?

(A) q   (B) π/p   (C) π/q   (D) 2π/p   (E) 2π/q

12. For the function defined by f(x) = A·cos(Bx + C) + D, coefficients A, B, C and D are all real numbers greater than

2. Increasing D would effect which of the following attributes of f(x)?

(A) Period and frequency only   (B) Period, frequency and phase shift only   (C) Amplitude only

(D) Vertical shift only   (E) Horizontal (phase) shift only

13. If $f(x) = \dfrac{5x-1}{3x} + \dfrac{1}{2}$ then $f^{-1}(x) = ?$

(A) $\dfrac{13x-2}{6x}$ (B) $\dfrac{-2}{13-6x}$ (C) $\dfrac{2}{13-6x}$ (D) $\dfrac{2}{6-13x}$ (E) $\dfrac{2}{13x-6}$

14. In a discount store that sells hardware equipments, a promotion goes as follows: "Buy four of the same item, pay for three only." What is the discount rate in this promotion?

(A) 20%   (B) 25%   (C) 30%   (D) 33%   (E) 40%

15. Angle AOB is in standard position and its terminal ray passes through the point (–2, –7). Which of the following can be the degree measure of an angle that is co – terminal with this angle?

(A) –254°   (B) –106°   (C) 196°   (D) 245 °   (E) 255°

16. For two positive integers a and b, it is given that $a^2 - 3ab - 4b^2 = 0$. What is the minimum possible value of a + b?

(A) 1   (B) 2   (C) 3   (D) 4   (E) 5

17. The table given shows the sales of a record recently released by Rush'n Sing Music Production in the first 6 months after the release. Which of the following best approximates the ratio of the number of copies sold in the 2nd month to that in the 5th month?

(A) 1.29   (B) 1.71   (C) 12.7   (D) 12.9   (E) 17.1

	Total Number of Copies Sold
End of 1st Month	8, 345
End of 2nd Month	12, 546
End of 3rd Month	14, 876
End of 4th Month	15, 997
End of 5th Month	16, 242
End of 6th Month	16, 456

18. For a parabola given by f(x) it is known that f(–2) = f(10). Which of the following can be the graph of f(x)?

(A)	(B)	(C)	(D)	(E)

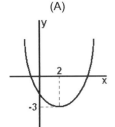
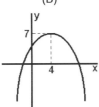
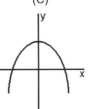
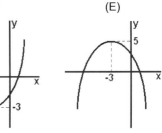

19. A relation β is given by $\{(x,y): 2x+3y=5; (x,y) \in R^2\}$; which of the following ordered pairs (x, y) is an element of both β and β^{-1}?

(A) (–5, 5)   (B) (–2, 3)   (C) (1, 1)   (D) (4, –1)
(E) None of the above

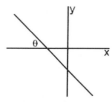

20. For the line given in figure 16, which of the following is correct about angle θ?

(A) tanθ = 1   (B) tanθ < 0   (C) tanθ < –1   (D) tanθ = 0   (E) tanθ > 0

Figure 16

21. A function f(x) has the property that $f(x_2) \geq f(x_1)$ when $x_2 > x_1$; which of the following can be the graph of f(x)?

(A)   (B)   (C)   (D)   (E)

22. The sculpture given in figure 17 is made of a hemisphere that sits on a 8 x 8 x 1 rectangular block where all dimensions are given in inches. If the surface area of the sculpture including all exposed faces as well as the square base not shown is 188.27 square inches then what is the volume occupied by the sculpture rounded to the nearest 10 cubic inches?

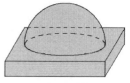

(A) 110   (B) 120   (C) 130   (D) 140

Figure 17

(E) It cannot be determined from the information given.

23. The points A(1, 3), B(0, 2) and C(–2, –5) are on a function y = f(x). Which of the following points must lie on y = f(–|x|)?

I. (–1, 3)   II. (2, –5)   III. (0, –2)

(A) I only   (B) II only   (C) III only   (D) I and II only   (E) I, II and III

24. A function g(x) is defined in terms of a polynomial function f(x) as $g(x) = \dfrac{f(x) + f(-x)}{2}$. Which of the following can be g(x)?

(A) $x^3 - x$ (B) $x^3 - x^2$ (C) $x^2 - 2x$ (D) $x^3 + x$ (E) $x^2 - 2$

25. Which of the following polar equations does not represent a circle?

(A) r = 2   (B) r = sinθ   (C) r = cosθ   (D) r = 1 + sinθ   (E) r = sinθ + cosθ

26. Suppose we have a calculator that can perform the operations of addition, subtraction, multiplication, division, square root and no other operation whatsoever. The calculator can carry out each operation correct to 8 decimal digits and can display no more than 16 digits. With this calculator, we would like to compute the value of the irrational number given by $\sqrt[4]{987^3}$ correct to the nearest hundredth decimal digit. What is the least number of operations that we must perform with this calculator if we wish to carry out every calculation using this calculator using pen and paper for recording the intermediate results only?

(A) 1   (B) 2   (C) 3   (D) 4   (E) More than 4

27. The graph of $y = 2 \cdot \csc(3x)$ is partially given in figure 18. What are the coordinates of point P?

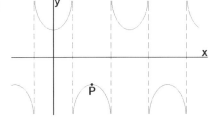

(A) $\left(\dfrac{\pi}{2}, -2\right)$ (B) $\left(\dfrac{2\pi}{3}, -2\right)$ (C) $\left(\dfrac{\pi}{3}, -2\right)$

(D) $\left(\dfrac{\pi}{3}, -1\right)$ (E) $\left(\dfrac{\pi}{3}, -\dfrac{1}{2}\right)$

Figure 18

28. If all points (x, y) that belong to the rectangular region given in figure 19 are transformed by the mapping(–2x, x + y), then the rectangle transforms into

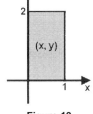

(A) a triangle   (B) a rhombus   (C) a parallelogram

(D) a square   (E) two triangles

Figure 19

29. What is the sum of the first n positive even integers in terms of n?

(A) $n^2 + n$ (B) $n^2 + 1$ (C) n^2 (D) $n^2 - 1$ (E) $n^2 - n$

30. According to the rule of 72, if a quantity grows at r% per year, then the doubling time is approximately $\dfrac{72}{r}$ years. $3000 is invested at the annual rate of 8% and we would like to calculate the time needed for the money to become $6000. What will be the error percentage when we perform the calculation by the rule of 72?

(A) 0.0178   (B) 0.0718   (C) 0.0781   (D) 7.18   (E) 7.81

31. When three consecutive positive integers are multiplied, what is the probability that the units digit of the product will be nonzero?

(A) 0.2   (B) 0.4   (C) 0.6   (D) 0.8

(E) It cannot be determined from the information given.

32. One side of the base of the right square pyramid given in figure 20 has a length of 10 inches and the pyramid occupies a volume of 400 cubic inches. What is the surface area of the pyramid in square inches?

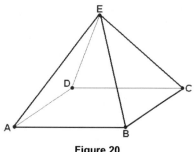

Figure 20

(A) 100   (B) 260   (C) 300   (D) 360   (E) 400

33. For a real polynomial P(x), P(−1) = P(1) = P(2) = 0. Which of the following is not necessarily a factor of P(x)?

(A) $x^2 - x - 2$ (B) $2 - x$ (C) $x^2 - 3x + 2$ (D) $x^2 - 1$ (E) $x^2 + x - 2$

34. In figure 21, PB bisects angle QPR. If $\dfrac{a}{b} = \dfrac{3}{4}$ then which of the following equals $\dfrac{q}{r}$?

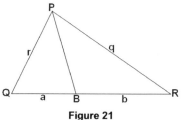

Figure 21

(A) $\dfrac{9}{16}$ (B) $\dfrac{3}{4}$ (C) $\dfrac{4}{3}$ (D) $\dfrac{16}{9}$

(E) It cannot be determined from the information given.

35. Which of the following can be the graph of a fourth degree polynomial function?

I.

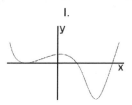

II.

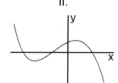

III.

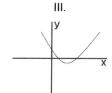

(A) I only   (B) II only   (C) III only   (D) I and III only   (E) I, II and III

36. If x and y are both integers then for how many ordered pairs (x, y) is it true that y = 0.4x and y is between 9 and 17?

(A) 2   (B) 4   (C) 6   (D) 7   (E) 20

37. If $A = \begin{bmatrix} 2 & a \\ a & -4 \end{bmatrix}$ and $B = \begin{bmatrix} 5 & -2 \\ -2 & 17 \end{bmatrix}$ then for which of the following values of a does $A^2 = B$?

(A) −2   (B) −1   (C) 0   (D) 1   (E) 2

38. If the infinite series $1 + \cos x + \cos^2 x + \cos^3 x + \cos^4 x + \dots$ converges to 2, then which of the following can be the degree measure of x?

(A) 30°   (B) 60°   (C) 90°   (D) 120°   (E) 135°

39. When a new integer is added to a list of 100 integers, which of the following can decrease?

I. range   II. median   III. standard deviation

(A) I only   (B) II only   (C) III only   (D) I and III only   (E) II and III only

40. The graph of the hyperbola defined by $\dfrac{x^2}{25} - \dfrac{y^2}{16} = 1$ is given in figure 22. If

the foci are located at points P and Q, then PD – QD = ?

(A) 5   (B) 10   (C) 25   (D) 50

(E) It cannot be determined from the information given.

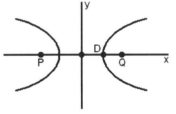

Figure 22

41. If in figure 23, BC bisects ACD, then what is the area of triangle BCD?

(A) 21   (B) 22.5   (C) 24   (D) 25

(E) It cannot be determined from the information given.

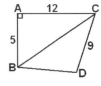

Figure 23

Figure not drawn to scale

42. The lifespan of a particular insect is normally distributed with the mean and the standard deviation of 66 and 4.4 hours respectively. What percent of such insects can be expected to have a longer lifespan than 70 hours?

(A) 15   (B) 16   (C) 17   (D) 18   (E) 19

43. Which of the following functions have the same zeros?

(A) sinx and cosx   (B) cosx and secx   (C) cosx and cotx   (D) tanx and cotx   (E) sinx and secx

44. As the positive real number x approaches 0, the function $\dfrac{e^{2x} - 1}{e^x - 1}$ approaches what number?

(A) –2   (B) –1   (C) 0   (D) 1   (E) 2

45. In figure 24, point A has the x coordinate of 4 and point B which lies on the parabola given by $y = 2x^2$ is closest to point A. What is the y coordinate of point B?

(A) 0.47   (B) 0.5   (C) 0.55   (D) 0.74   (E) 1.099

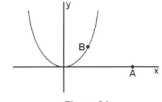

Figure 24

46. If x and y are two integers then for how many distinct ordered pairs (x, y) does the inequality given by $x^2 + y^2 \le 5$ hold?

(A) 8   (B) 10   (C) 12   (D) 16   (E) More than 16

47. A periodic function y = f(x) whose graph is partially given in figure 25 has a period of T and it satisfies the relation $f(x - T/2) = -f(x)$; such a function is said to have "quarter wave symmetry". Which of the following correctly gives one period of this function?

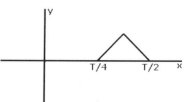

Figure 25

(A)

(B)

(C)

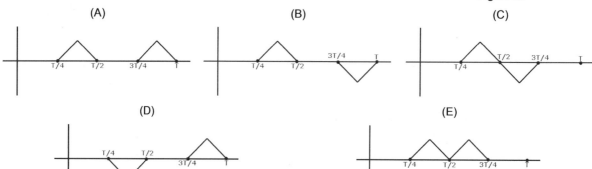

(D)

(E)

48. The line given by the equation $\dfrac{x-3}{2} = \dfrac{y-4}{3} = \dfrac{z}{-2}$ is reflected across the xy plane. Which of the following can be the equation of the line that results?

(A) $\dfrac{x+3}{2} = \dfrac{y+4}{3} = \dfrac{z}{-2}$

(B) $\dfrac{x-3}{2} = \dfrac{y-4}{3} = \dfrac{z}{2}$

(C) $\dfrac{x-3}{4} = \dfrac{y-4}{9} = \dfrac{z}{-4}$

(D) $\dfrac{x-3}{-2} = \dfrac{y-4}{-3} = \dfrac{z}{2}$

(E) $\dfrac{x+3}{2} = \dfrac{y+4}{3} = \dfrac{z}{2}$

49. Which of the following is the exact value of x^n if x = 2.01 and n = 5?
(A) 32.8080401001
(B) 32.8080401010
(C) 32.8080401011
(D) 32.8080401101
(E) 32.8080401111

50. In figure 26, points A, B, C and D are 4 consecutive vertices of the partially given 9 sided polygon which is both convex and regular. What is the ratio of the length of side AD to the length of side BD in the shaded triangle?

(A) 1.2 (B) 1.3 (C) 1.4 (D) 1.5 (E) 1.6

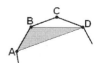

Figure 26

S T O P
END OF TEST

Answer Keys to the Model Tests:

Answer Key to SAT Math Level 1 – Model Test	
1. **B**	26. **A**
2. **C**	27. **A**
3. **B**	28. **C**
4. **A**	29. **E**
5. **A**	30. **C**
6. **A**	31. **E**
7. **B**	32. **C**
8. **D**	33. **D**
9. **D**	34. **C**
10. **C**	35. **C**
11. **C**	36. **C**
12. **C**	37. **C**
13. **D**	38. **C**
14. **D**	39. **C**
15. **B**	40. **D**
16. **D**	41. **E**
17. **D**	42. **D**
18. **C**	43. **A**
19. **C**	44. **C**
20. **C**	45. **A**
21. **D**	46. **A**
22. **B**	47. **E**
23. **C**	48. **A**
24. **B**	49. **C**
25. **B**	50. **B**

Answer Key to SAT Math Level 2 – Model Test	
1. **A**	26. **C**
2. **C**	27. **A**
3. **C**	28. **C**
4. **D**	29. **A**
5. **B**	30. **B**
6. **D**	31. **B**
7. **A**	32. **D**
8. **B**	33. **E**
9. **C**	34. **C**
10. **D**	35. **D**
11. **E**	36. **B**
12. **D**	37. **D**
13. **C**	38. **B**
14. **B**	39. **E**
15. **B**	40. **B**
16. **E**	41. **B**
17. **E**	42. **D**
18. **B**	43. **C**
19. **C**	44. **E**
20. **E**	45. **E**
21. **A**	46. **E**
22. **B**	47. **B**
23. **B**	48. **B**
24. **E**	49. **A**
25. **D**	50. **B**

Scaled Score Conversion Table SAT Mathematics Level 1 Subject Test					
Raw Score	Scaled Score	Raw Score	Scaled Score	Raw Score	Scaled Score
50	800	28	590	6	390
49	790	27	580	5	380
48	780	26	570	4	380
47	780	25	560	3	370
46	770	24	550	2	360
45	750	23	540	1	350
44	740	22	530	0	340
43	740	21	520	−1	340
42	730	20	510	−2	330
41	720	19	500	−3	320
40	710	18	490	−4	310
39	710	17	480	−5	300
38	700	16	470	−6	280
37	690	15	460	−7	270
36	680	14	460	−8	260
35	670	13	450	−9	260
34	660	12	440	−10	250
33	650	11	430	−11	240
32	640	10	420		
31	630	9	420		
30	620	8	410		
29	600	7	400		

Scaled Score Conversion Table SAT Mathematics Level 2 Subject Test					
Raw Score	Scaled Score	Raw Score	Scaled Score	Raw Score	Scaled Score
50	800	28	650	6	480
49	800	27	640	5	470
48	800	26	630	4	460
47	800	25	630	3	450
46	800	24	620	2	440
45	800	23	610	1	430
44	800	22	600	0	410
43	800	21	590	−1	390
42	790	20	580	−2	370
41	780	19	570	−3	360
40	770	18	560	−4	340
39	760	17	560	−5	340
38	750	16	550	−6	330
37	740	15	540	−7	320
36	730	14	530	−8	320
35	720	13	530	−9	320
34	710	12	520	−10	320
33	700	11	510	−11	310
32	690	10	500	−12	310
31	680	9	500		
30	670	8	490		
29	660	7	480		

INDEX

If you can fill the unforgiving minute
With sixty seconds' worth of distance run…
Rudyard KIPLING

If you would create something,you must be something.

Johann Wolfgang VON GOETHE

Made in the USA
Lexington, KY
13 May 2013